FOUNDATION ATLAS

First published 1998, reprinted 1998, 1999 (twice), 2000

Revised edition 2001, reprinted 2002, 2003

© Collins-Longman Atlases 1998, 2001

The maps in this atlas are licensed to Collins-Longman Atlases
and are derived from databases © HarperCollins Publishers.

HarperCollins Publishers, Westerhill Road, Bishopbriggs, Glasgow G64 2QT

Pearson Education Ltd, Edinburgh Gate, Harlow, Essex CM20 2JE
ISBN 0-00-712007-9

Cover photograph: Images Colour Library
Cover design: The Image Works

Printed in Singapore

QL11562

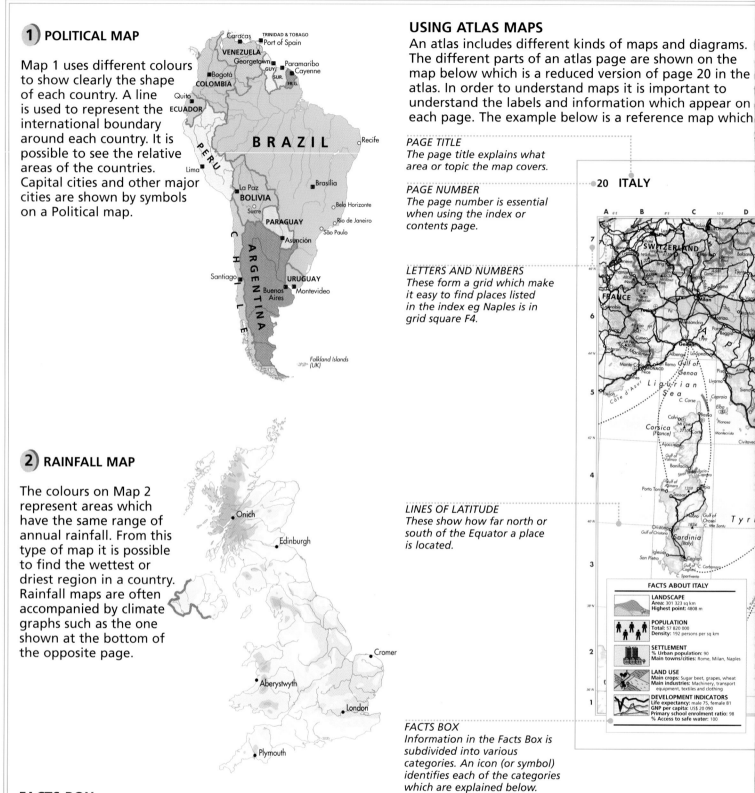

1 POLITICAL MAP

Map 1 uses different colours to show clearly the shape of each country. A line is used to represent the international boundary around each country. It is possible to see the relative areas of the countries. Capital cities and other major cities are shown by symbols on a Political map.

2 RAINFALL MAP

The colours on Map 2 represent areas which have the same range of annual rainfall. From this type of map it is possible to find the wettest or driest region in a country. Rainfall maps are often accompanied by climate graphs such as the one shown at the bottom of the opposite page.

USING ATLAS MAPS

An atlas includes different kinds of maps and diagrams. The different parts of an atlas page are shown on the map below which is a reduced version of page 20 in the atlas. In order to understand maps it is important to understand the labels and information which appear on each page. The example below is a reference map which

PAGE TITLE
The page title explains what area or topic the map covers.

PAGE NUMBER
The page number is essential when using the index or contents page.

LETTERS AND NUMBERS
These form a grid which make it easy to find places listed in the index eg Naples is in grid square F4.

LINES OF LATITUDE
These show how far north or south of the Equator a place is located.

FACTS BOX
Information in the Facts Box is subdivided into various categories. An icon (or symbol) identifies each of the categories which are explained below.

20   ITALY

FACTS ABOUT ITALY

LANDSCAPE
Area: 301 323 sq km
Highest point: 4808 m

POPULATION
Total: 57 820 000
Density: 192 persons per sq km

SETTLEMENT
% Urban population: 90
Main towns/cities: Rome, Milan, Naples

LAND USE
Main crops: Sugar beet, grapes, wheat
Main industries: Machinery, transport
  equipment, textiles and clothing

DEVELOPMENT INDICATORS
Life expectancy: male 75, female 81
GNP per capita: US$ 20 090
Primary school enrolment ratio: 98
% Access to safe water: 100

FACTS BOX...

The information listed in the FACTS ABOUT... box is explained below.

LANDSCAPE: Indicates the area and highest point.

POPULATION: Lists the total population and the average number of people living in one square kilometre.

SETTLEMENT: Shows the percentage of the population living in cities and towns. The main towns and cities are also listed.

LAND USE: Main crops grown and the main industries in the region are identified here.

DEVELOPMENT INDICATORS: Four indicators are shown here

Life expectancy: The number of years a newborn child can expect to survive.

GNP per capita: The annual value of production of goods and services of a country, per person.

Primary school enrolment: The total of all ages enrolled at primary level as a percentage of primary age children.

Access to safe water: Percentage of the population with reasonable access to sufficient safe water.

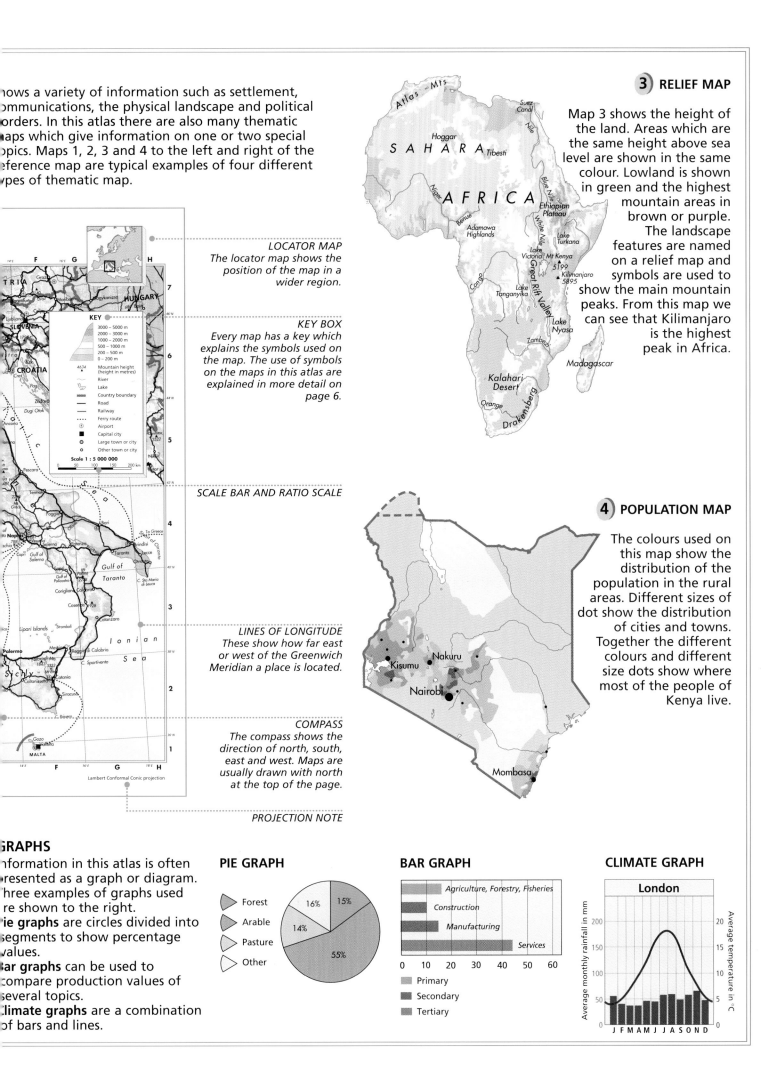

...ows a variety of information such as settlement, ...ommunications, the physical landscape and political ...orders. In this atlas there are also many thematic ...aps which give information on one or two special ...pics. Maps 1, 2, 3 and 4 to the left and right of the ...eference map are typical examples of four different ...pes of thematic map.

LOCATOR MAP
The locator map shows the position of the map in a wider region.

KEY

	3000 – 5000 m
	2000 – 3000 m
	1000 – 2000 m
	500 – 1000 m
	200 – 500 m
	0 – 200 m
▲ 4634	Mountain height (height in metres)
	River
	Lake
	Country boundary
	Road
	Railway
	Ferry route
⊕	Airport
■	Capital city
◎	Large town or city
○	Other town or city

Scale 1 : 5 000 000

KEY BOX
Every map has a key which explains the symbols used on the map. The use of symbols on the maps in this atlas are explained in more detail on page 6.

SCALE BAR AND RATIO SCALE

LINES OF LONGITUDE
These show how far east or west of the Greenwich Meridian a place is located.

COMPASS
The compass shows the direction of north, south, east and west. Maps are usually drawn with north at the top of the page.

Lambert Conformal Conic projection

PROJECTION NOTE

3) RELIEF MAP

Map 3 shows the height of the land. Areas which are the same height above sea level are shown in the same colour. Lowland is shown in green and the highest mountain areas in brown or purple. The landscape features are named on a relief map and symbols are used to show the main mountain peaks. From this map we can see that Kilimanjaro is the highest peak in Africa.

4) POPULATION MAP

The colours used on this map show the distribution of the population in the rural areas. Different sizes of dot show the distribution of cities and towns. Together the different colours and different size dots show where most of the people of Kenya live.

GRAPHS

Information in this atlas is often presented as a graph or diagram. Three examples of graphs used are shown to the right.

Pie graphs are circles divided into segments to show percentage values.

Bar graphs can be used to compare production values of several topics.

Climate graphs are a combination of bars and lines.

PIE GRAPH

15%
16%
14%
55%

▷ Forest
▷ Arable
▷ Pasture
▷ Other

BAR GRAPH

Agriculture, Forestry, Fisheries
Construction
Manufacturing
Services

0 10 20 30 40 50 60

■ Primary
■ Secondary
■ Tertiary

CLIMATE GRAPH

London

Average monthly rainfall in mm
200
150
100
50
0

Average temperature in °C
20
15
10
5
0

J F M A M J J A S O N D

LATITUDE AND LONGITUDE

Lines of latitude are imaginary lines which run in an east-west direction around the globe. They run parallel to each other and are measured in degrees, written as °. The most important line of latitude is the **Equator**, 0°. All other lines of latitude have a value between 0° and 90° North or South of the Equator. 90° north is the North Pole and, 90° south, the South Pole.

Lines of longitude are imaginary lines which run in a north-south direction between the **North Pole** and the **South Pole**. The most important line of longitude is 0°, the **Greenwich Meridian**, which runs through the Greenwich Observatory in London. Exactly opposite the Greenwich Meridian on the other side of the world, is the 180° line of longitude. All other lines of longitude are measured in degrees east or west of 0°.

When both lines of latitude and longitude are drawn on a map they form a grid. It is easy to find a place on the map if the latitude and longitude values are known. The point of intersection of the line of latitude and the line of longitude locates the place exactly.

The Equator can be used to divide the globe into two halves. Land north of the Equator is the **Northern Hemisphere.** Land south of the Equator is the **Southern Hemisphere.** The 0° and 180° lines of longitude can also be used to divide the globe into two halves, the **Western** and **Eastern Hemispheres.** Together, the Equator and 0° and 180°, divide the world into four areas, for example, North America is in the Northern Hemisphere and the Western Hemisphere.

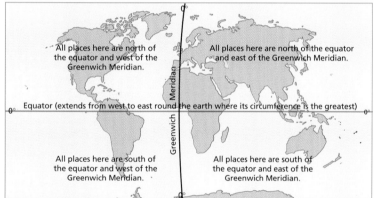

All places here are north of the equator and west of the Greenwich Meridian.

All places here are north of the equator and east of the Greenwich Meridian.

Equator (extends from west to east round the earth where its circumference is the greatest)

All places here are south of the equator and west of the Greenwich Meridian.

All places here are south of the equator and east of the Greenwich Meridian.

Greenwich Meridian

USING SCALE

The **scale** of each map in this atlas is shown in two ways:

1 The **Ratio scale** is written, for example, as 1 : 1 000 000. This means that one unit of measurement on the map represents 1 000 000 of the same unit on the ground.

eg **Scale 1 : 1 000 000**

2 The **line** or **bar scale** shows the scale as a line with the distance on the ground marked at intervals along the line.

0   10   20   30   40   50   60   70   80   90   100 km

DIFFERENT SCALES

The three maps to the right cover the same area of the page but are at different scales. Map A is a large scale map which shows a small area in detail. Map C is a small scale map which means it shows a larger area in the same space as Map A, however in much less detail. The area of MAP A is highlighted on maps B and C. As the scale ratio increases the map becomes smaller.

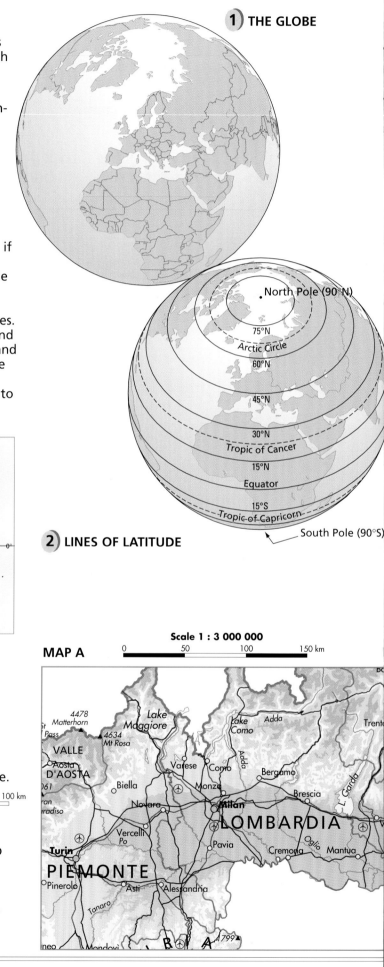

1 THE GLOBE

North Pole (90°N)

75°N

Arctic Circle

60°N

45°N

30°N

Tropic of Cancer

15°N

Equator

15°S

Tropic of Capricorn

South Pole (90°S)

2 LINES OF LATITUDE

MAP A

Scale 1 : 3 000 000

0   50   100   150 km

4478 Matterhorn
St Pass
4634 Mt Rosa
VALLE
D'AOSTA
Aosta
Gran Paradiso
061
Turin
PIEMONTE
Pinerolo
Tanaro
Lake Maggiore
Lake Como
Adda
Trento
Varese
Como
Bergamo
Biella
Monza
Brescia
L. Garda
Novara
Milan
Vercelli
Po
LOMBARDIA
Pavia
Cremona
Oglio
Mantua
Asti
Alessandria
neo
Mondovi
B   A
1799

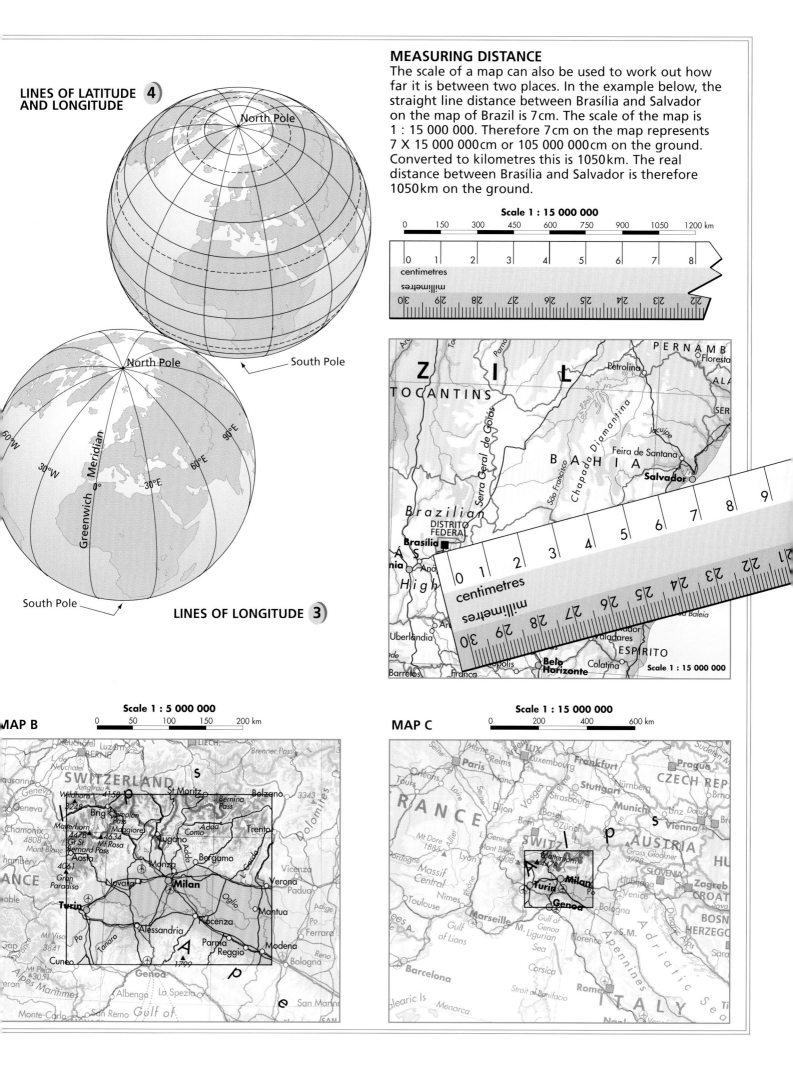

LINES OF LATITUDE AND LONGITUDE ④

North Pole

South Pole

LINES OF LONGITUDE ③

North Pole

60°W

30°W

Greenwich Meridian

0°

30°E

60°E

90°E

South Pole

MEASURING DISTANCE

The scale of a map can also be used to work out how far it is between two places. In the example below, the straight line distance between Brasília and Salvador on the map of Brazil is 7cm. The scale of the map is 1 : 15 000 000. Therefore 7cm on the map represents 7 X 15 000 000cm or 105 000 000cm on the ground. Converted to kilometres this is 1050km. The real distance between Brasília and Salvador is therefore 1050km on the ground.

Scale 1 : 15 000 000

0   150   300   450   600   750   900   1050   1200 km

Scale 1 : 5 000 000

MAP B

0   50   100   150   200 km

Scale 1 : 15 000 000

MAP C

0   200   400   600 km

SYMBOLS

Maps use **symbols** to show the location of a feature and to give information about that feature. The symbols used on each map in this atlas are explained in the **key** to each map.

Symbols used on maps can be dots, diagrams, lines or area colours. They vary in colour, size and shape. The captions to the map below help explain some of the symbols used on the maps in this atlas.

Different styles of type are also used to show differences between features, for example, country names are shown in large bold capitals, small water features, rivers and lakes in small italics.

USING GRIDS

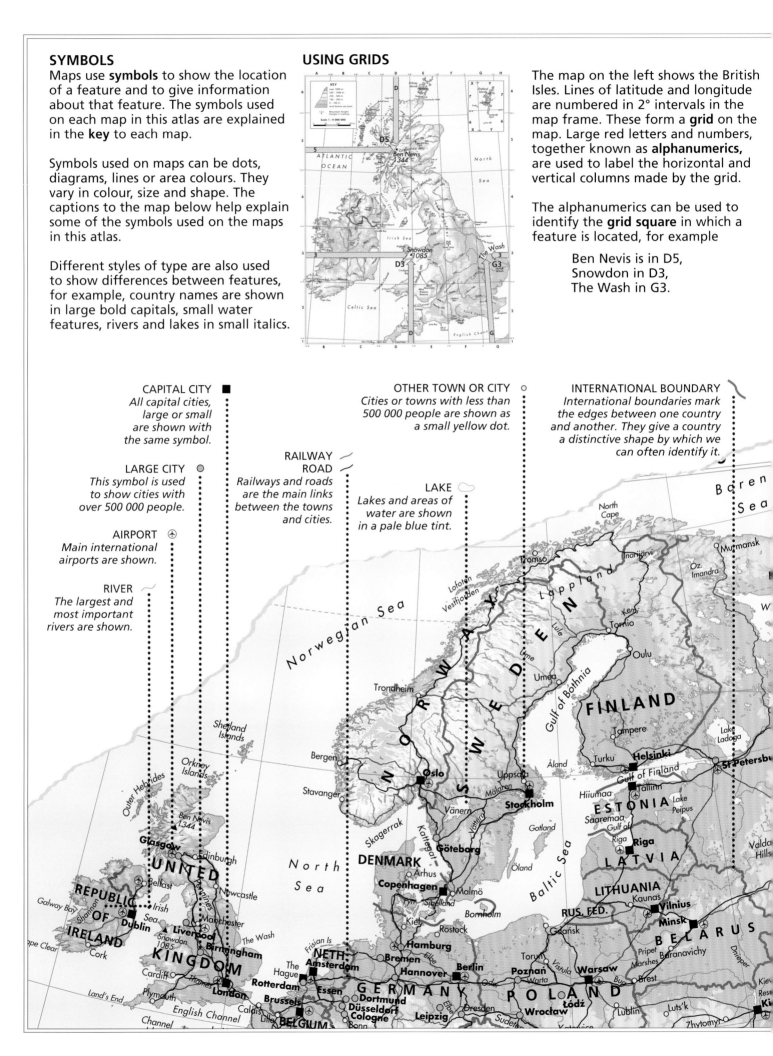

The map on the left shows the British Isles. Lines of latitude and longitude are numbered in 2° intervals in the map frame. These form a **grid** on the map. Large red letters and numbers, together known as **alphanumerics,** are used to label the horizontal and vertical columns made by the grid.

The alphanumerics can be used to identify the **grid square** in which a feature is located, for example

Ben Nevis is in D5,
Snowdon in D3,
The Wash in G3.

CAPITAL CITY ■
All capital cities, large or small are shown with the same symbol.

LARGE CITY ●
This symbol is used to show cities with over 500 000 people.

AIRPORT ⊕
Main international airports are shown.

RIVER
The largest and most important rivers are shown.

RAILWAY
ROAD
Railways and roads are the main links between the towns and cities.

OTHER TOWN OR CITY ○
Cities or towns with less than 500 000 people are shown as a small yellow dot.

LAKE
Lakes and areas of water are shown in a pale blue tint.

INTERNATIONAL BOUNDARY
International boundaries mark the edges between one country and another. They give a country a distinctive shape by which we can often identify it.

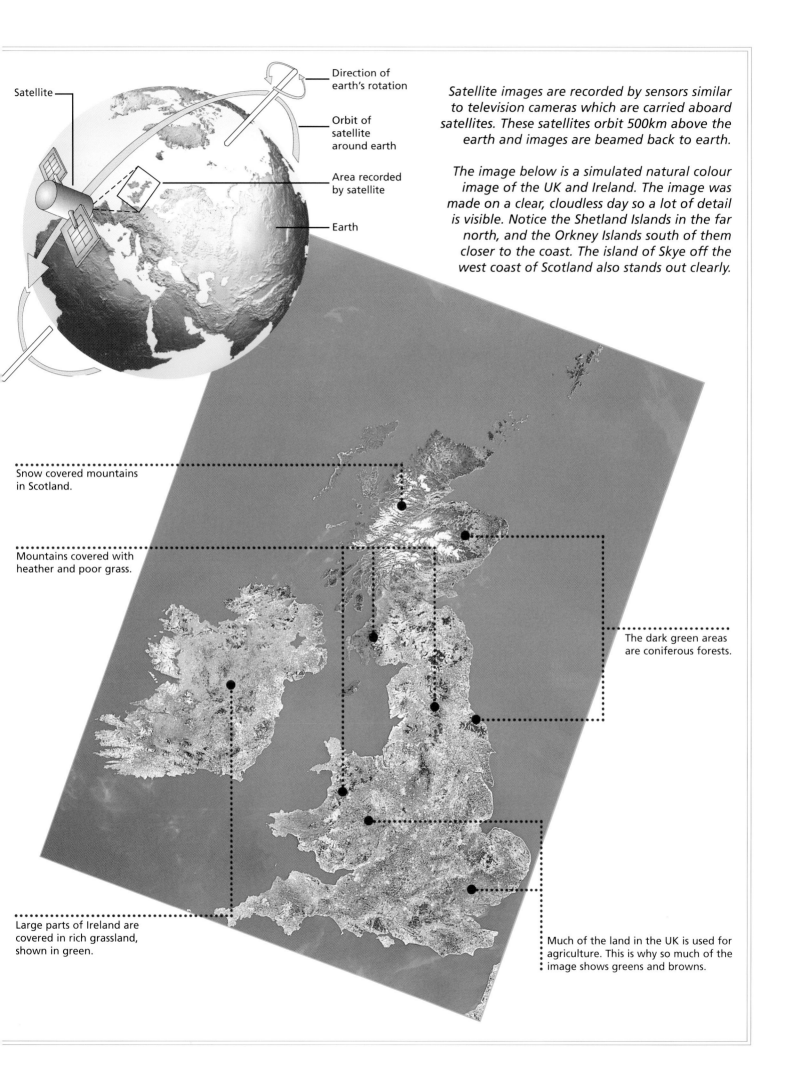

Satellite

Direction of earth's rotation

Orbit of satellite around earth

Area recorded by satellite

Earth

Satellite images are recorded by sensors similar to television cameras which are carried aboard satellites. These satellites orbit 500km above the earth and images are beamed back to earth.

The image below is a simulated natural colour image of the UK and Ireland. The image was made on a clear, cloudless day so a lot of detail is visible. Notice the Shetland Islands in the far north, and the Orkney Islands south of them closer to the coast. The island of Skye off the west coast of Scotland also stands out clearly.

Snow covered mountains in Scotland.

Mountains covered with heather and poor grass.

The dark green areas are coniferous forests.

Large parts of Ireland are covered in rich grassland, shown in green.

Much of the land in the UK is used for agriculture. This is why so much of the image shows greens and browns.

KEY

over 1000 m
500 – 1000 m
200 – 500 m
100 – 200 m
0 – 100 m
land below sea level

▲ 1344 Mountain height (height in metres)

Scale 1 : 4 000 000

0   50   100   150 km

ATLANTIC OCEAN

Outer Hebrides

Cape Wrath
Butt of Lewis
Lewis
Clisham 799
Harris
North Uist
South Uist
Barra
Skye
Rum
Coll
Tiree
Mull
Ben More 966
Inner Hebrides
Firth of Lorn
Jura
Islay
Arran

The Minch
North West Highlands
Loch Broom
Loch Ness
Ben Nevis 1344
Loch Awe
Loch Lomond
Loch Tay
Grampian Mts
Ben Lawers 1214
Cairngorm Mts
Ben Macdui 1309
Dee
Don
Spey
Toy
Ochil Hills
Firth of Tay
Forth
Firth of Forth

Orkney Islands
Mainland
Hoy
Pentland Firth
Duncansby Head
Dornoch Firth
Moray Firth

Firth of Clyde
Clyde

X   2°W   Y
Shetland Islands
7   Yell   7
Foula   Mainland
60°N   60°N
6   Sumburgh Head   6
Fair Isle
X   2°W   Y

North Sea

Southern Uplands
Merrick 843
Cheviot Hills
Tweed
Tyne
Solway Firth
Tees
The Pennines
Scafell Pike 977
Lake District
North York Moors
Flamborough Head
Morecambe Bay
Ribble
Derwent
Ouse
Mouth of the Humber
Spurn Head
Mersey
High Peak
Kinder Scout 636
The Wash

Malin Head
Errigal 752
Donegal Bay
Lough Conn
Achill
Lough Mask
Galway Bay
Lough Corrib
Lough Derg
Shannon
Lough Ree
Lough
Foyle
Bann
Lower Lough Erne
Upper Lough Erne
Erne
Antrim Mts
Lough Neagh
Lagan
Mourne Mts
Slieve Donard 852
Dundalk Bay
North Channel
Boyne
Liffey
Barrow
Suir
Blackwater
Lugnaquilla Mtn 926
Wicklow Mts
Shannon

Dingle B.
Carrantuohill 1041
Cape Clear

Isle of Man

Irish Sea

Anglesey
Caernarfon Bay
Snowdon 1085
Cambrian Mountains
Dee
Cardigan Bay
Teifi
Black Mountains
886
Breacon Beacons
Carmarthen Bay
St David's Head
St George's Channel

Celtic Sea

Trent
Severn
Avon
Wye
Severn
Avon
Mendip Hills
Salisbury Plain
Cotswold Hills
Thames
Chiltern Hills
Thames
North Downs
South Downs
The Fens
Great Ouse
Norfolk Broads
Dungeness
Beachy Head

Bristol Channel
Exmoor
New Forest
Isle of Wight
Bodmin Moor
Dartmoor
Yes Tor 619
Tamar
Exe
Lyme Bay
Bill of Portland
Isle of Scilly
Land's End
Lizard Point

English Channel

Conic Projection

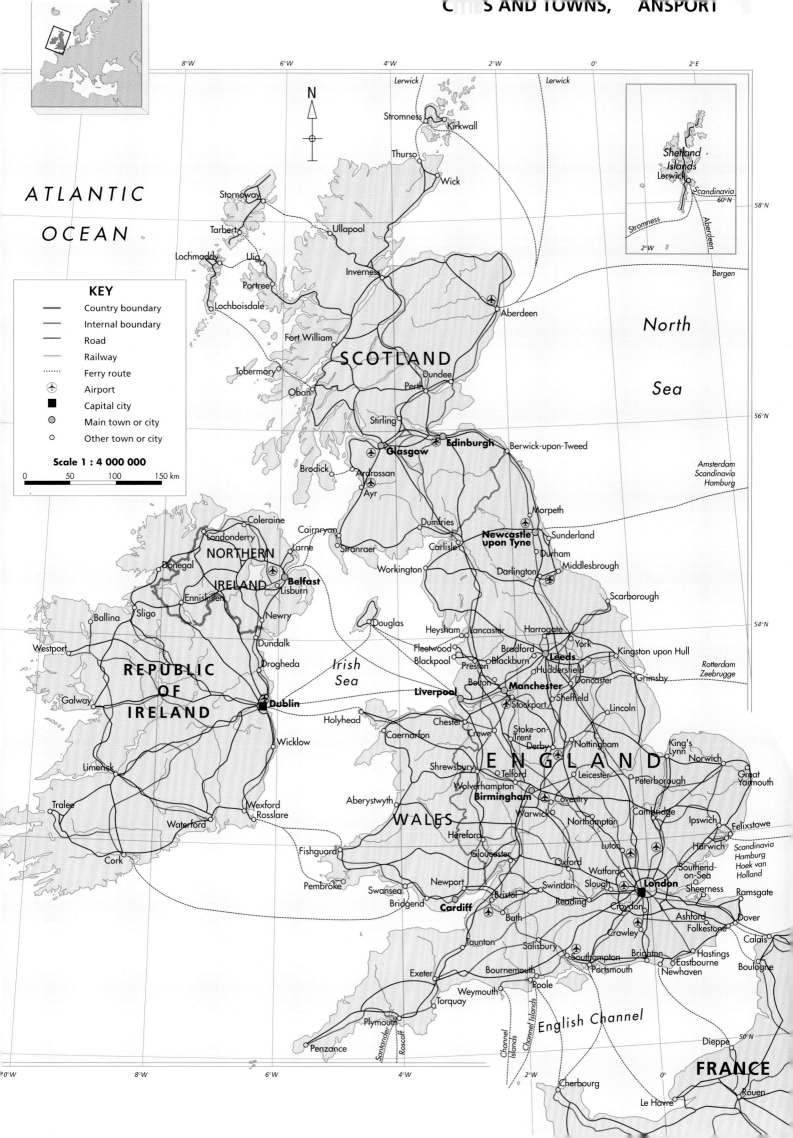

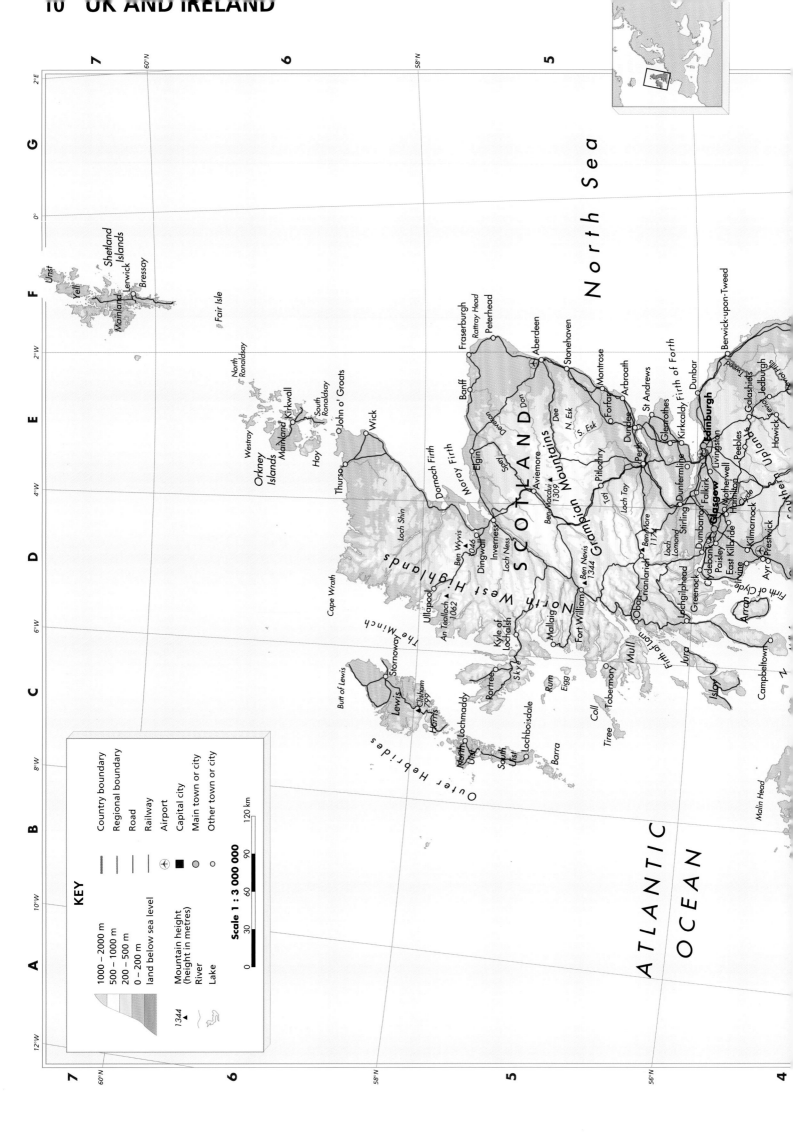

KEY

	Country boundary
	Regional boundary
	Road
	Railway
✈	Airport
■	Capital city
●	Main town or city
○	Other town or city

1000 – 2000 m
500 – 1000 m
200 – 500 m
0 – 200 m
land below sea level

▲ 1344 Mountain height (height in metres)
～ River
⌇ Lake

Scale 1 : 3 000 000

0   30   60   90   120 km

Shetland Islands

Unst
Yell
Mainland
Lerwick
Bressay

Fair Isle

North Ronaldsay

Westray
Orkney Islands
Mainland
Kirkwall
South Ronaldsay
Hoy

John o' Groats

Thurso
Wick

Dornoch Firth
Cape Wrath

Loch Shin

Moray Firth
Elgin
Banff
Fraserburgh
Rattray Head
Peterhead

North West Highlands
Ben Wyvis ▲ 1046
Dingwall
Inverness
Aviemore
Deveron
Spey
Findhorn
Dee
N. Esk
S. Esk

Aberdeen
Stonehaven
Montrose
Arbroath
Forfar

SCOTLAND
Ben Macdui ▲ 1309
Grampian Mountains
Loch Tay
Loch Ness
Loch

Dundee
St Andrews
Perth
Pitlochry
Tay

Butt of Lewis
Stornoway
Lewis
Clisham ▲ 799
Harris
The Minch

Outer Hebrides

North Uist
Lochmaddy
South Uist
Lochboisdale
Barra

Ullapool
An Teallach ▲ 1062

Kyle of Lochalsh
Portree
Skye
Rum
Eigg

Mallaig
Fort William
Ben Nevis ▲ 1344

Coll
Tiree
Mull
Tobermory
Firth of Lorn
Jura

Oban
Crianlarich
Ben More ▲ 1174
Loch Lomond
Lochgilphead
Dumbarton
Clydebank
Greenock
Paisley

Islay
Campbeltown

Stirling
Falkirk
Glasgow
Hamilton
East Kilbride
Motherwell
Kilmarnock
Clyde
Arran
Firth of Clyde
Ayr
Prestwick
Irvine

Dunfermline
Kirkcaldy Firth of Forth
Glenrothes
Edinburgh
Livingston
Peebles
Southern Uplands
Galashiels
Jedburgh
Hawick
Tweed
Berwick-upon-Tweed

Dunbar

North Sea

Malin Head

ATLANTIC OCEAN

58°N
56°N
60°N

12°W 10°W 8°W 6°W 4°W 2°W 0 2°E

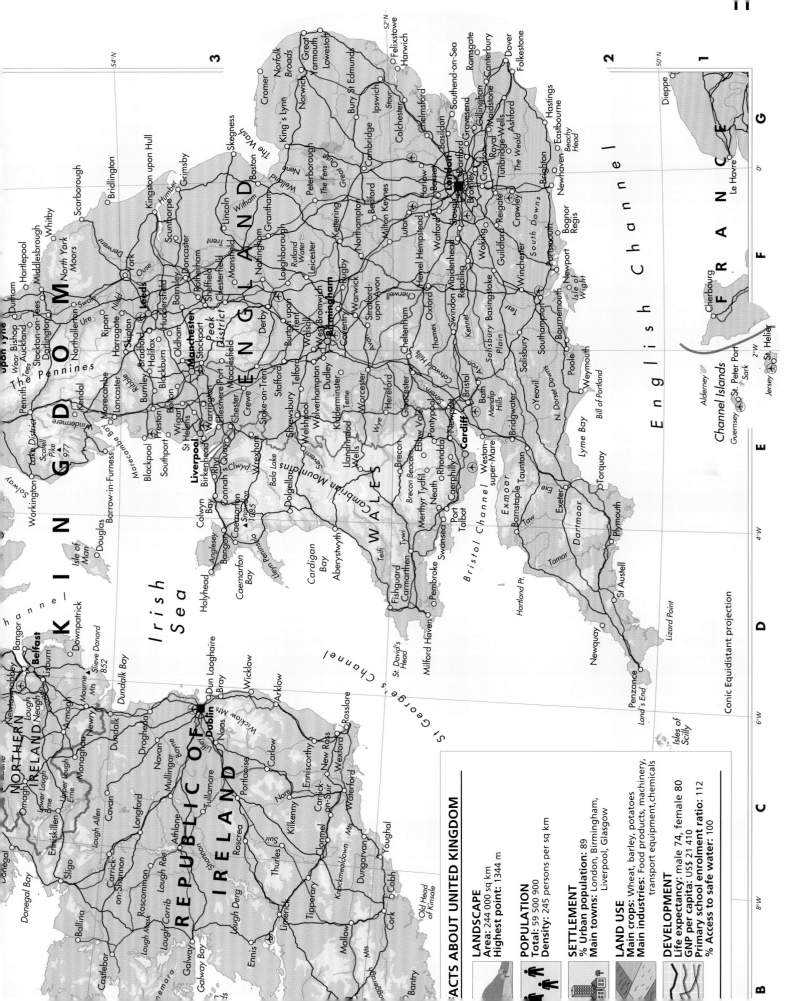

FACTS ABOUT UNITED KINGDOM

LANDSCAPE
Area: 244 000 sq km
Highest point: 1344 m

POPULATION
Total: 59 500 900
Density: 245 persons per sq km

SETTLEMENT
% Urban population: 89
Main towns: London, Birmingham, Liverpool, Glasgow

LAND USE
Main crops: Wheat, barley, potatoes
Main industries: Food products, machinery, transport equipment, chemicals

DEVELOPMENT
Life expectancy: male 74, female 80
GNP per capita: US$ 21 410
Primary school enrolment ratio: 112
% Access to safe water: 100

Conic Equidistant projection

ANNUAL RAINFALL

There is little variation between winter and summer. The highest rainfall is in the west where winds from the sea blow against the mountains and hills. Central and eastern areas are more sheltered and have lower rainfall.

CLIMATE GRAPHS AND STATISTICS

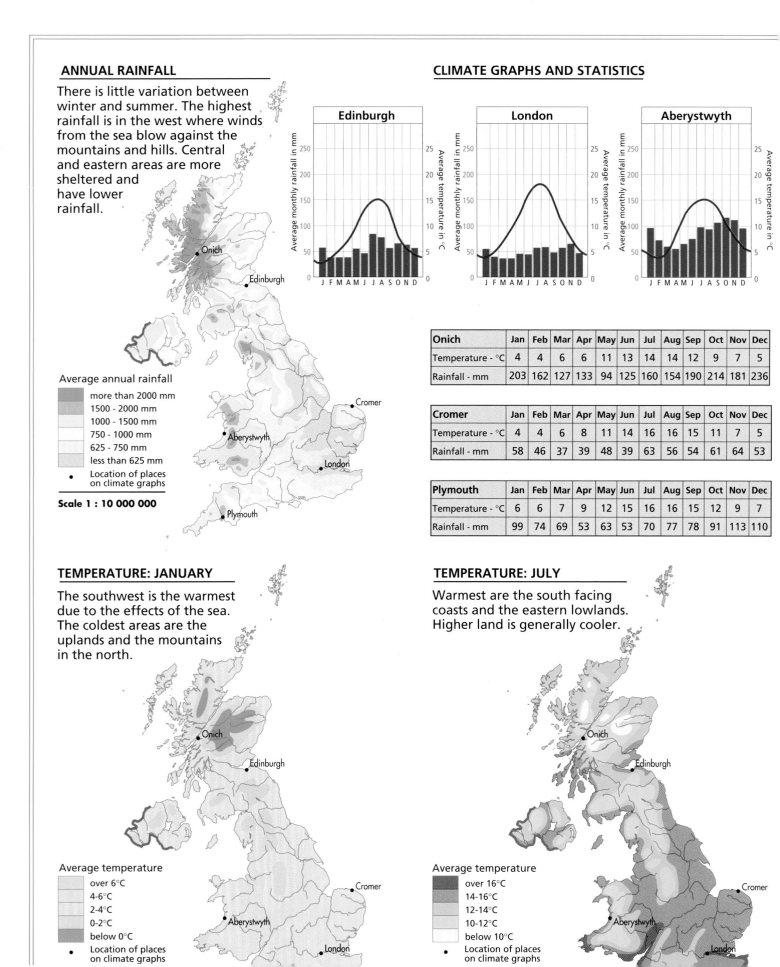

Average annual rainfall

- more than 2000 mm
- 1500 - 2000 mm
- 1000 - 1500 mm
- 750 - 1000 mm
- 625 - 750 mm
- less than 625 mm
- • Location of places on climate graphs

Scale 1 : 10 000 000

Onich	Jan	Feb	Mar	Apr	May	Jun	Jul	Aug	Sep	Oct	Nov	Dec
Temperature - °C	4	4	6	6	11	13	14	14	12	9	7	5
Rainfall - mm	203	162	127	133	94	125	160	154	190	214	181	236

Cromer	Jan	Feb	Mar	Apr	May	Jun	Jul	Aug	Sep	Oct	Nov	Dec
Temperature - °C	4	4	6	8	11	14	16	16	15	11	7	5
Rainfall - mm	58	46	37	39	48	39	63	56	54	61	64	53

Plymouth	Jan	Feb	Mar	Apr	May	Jun	Jul	Aug	Sep	Oct	Nov	Dec
Temperature - °C	6	6	7	9	12	15	16	16	15	12	9	7
Rainfall - mm	99	74	69	53	63	53	70	77	78	91	113	110

TEMPERATURE: JANUARY

The southwest is the warmest due to the effects of the sea. The coldest areas are the uplands and the mountains in the north.

Average temperature

- over 6°C
- 4-6°C
- 2-4°C
- 0-2°C
- below 0°C
- • Location of places on climate graphs

TEMPERATURE: JULY

Warmest are the south facing coasts and the eastern lowlands. Higher land is generally cooler.

Average temperature

- over 16°C
- 14-16°C
- 12-14°C
- 10-12°C
- below 10°C
- • Location of places on climate graphs

POPULATION DENSITY

The greatest concentration of population in the
United Kingdom is found in the areas immediately
surrounding London where the number of persons
per square kilometre is more than 500 times
greater than in the Scottish Highlands. The total
population of England is greater than the sum of
the populations of Scotland, Wales and Northern
Ireland.

Persons per sq. km

over 150
10 - 150
less than 10

Cities and towns

● over 1 000 000
● 500 000 - 1 000 000
● 100 000 - 500 000
• 25 000 - 100 000

Scale 1 : 5 000 000

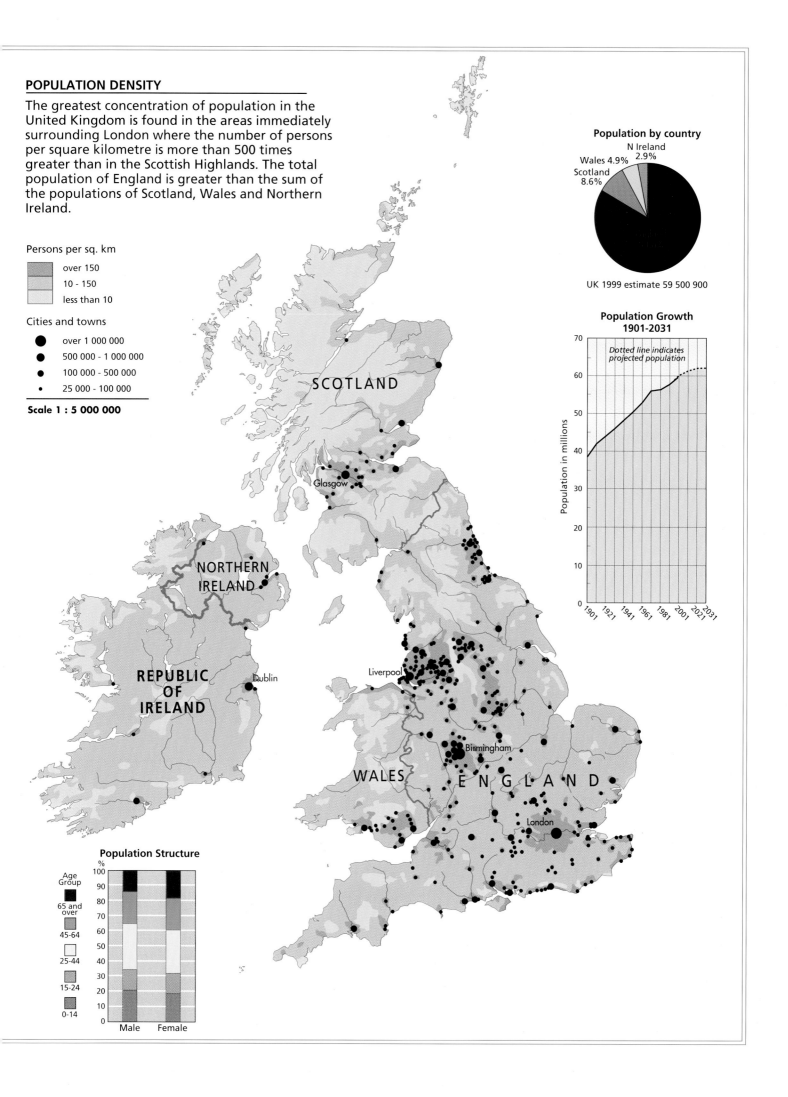

Population by country

N Ireland
2.9%
Wales 4.9%
Scotland
8.6%

UK 1999 estimate 59 500 900

**Population Growth
1901-2031**

*Dotted line indicates
projected population*

Population in millions

70
60
50
40
30
20
10
0

1901 1921 1941 1961 1981 2001 2021 2031

SCOTLAND

Glasgow

NORTHERN
IRELAND

REPUBLIC
OF
IRELAND

Dublin

Liverpool

Birmingham

WALES   E N G L A N D

London

Population Structure

%
100
90
80
70
60
50
40
30
20
10
0

Age
Group

65 and
over

45-64

25-44

15-24

0-14

Male   Female

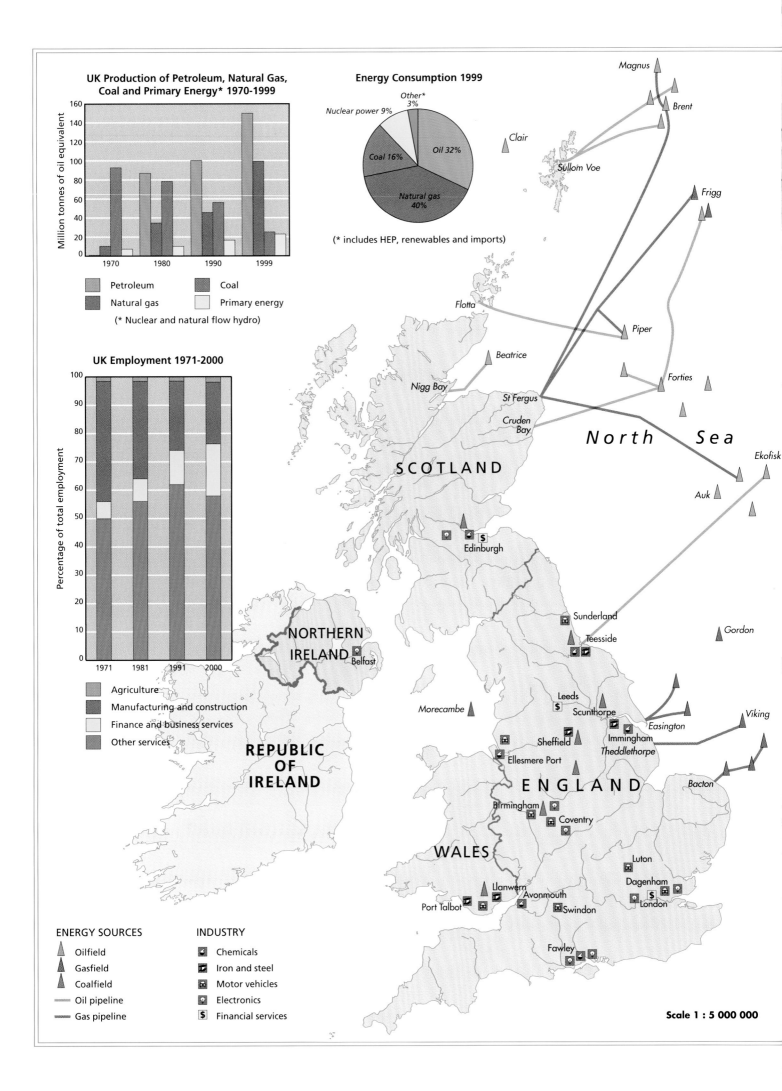

UK Production of Petroleum, Natural Gas, Coal and Primary Energy* 1970-1999

Million tonnes of oil equivalent

- Petroleum
- Natural gas
- Coal
- Primary energy

(* Nuclear and natural flow hydro)

Energy Consumption 1999

- Nuclear power 9%
- Other* 3%
- Oil 32%
- Coal 16%
- Natural gas 40%

(* includes HEP, renewables and imports)

UK Employment 1971-2000

Percentage of total employment

- Agriculture
- Manufacturing and construction
- Finance and business services
- Other services

ENERGY SOURCES
- ▲ Oilfield
- ▲ Gasfield
- ▲ Coalfield
- — Oil pipeline
- — Gas pipeline

INDUSTRY
- Chemicals
- Iron and steel
- Motor vehicles
- Electronics
- $ Financial services

Scale 1 : 5 000 000

North Sea

Magnus
Brent
Clair
Sullom Voe
Frigg
Flotta
Piper
Beatrice
Nigg Bay
St Fergus
Cruden Bay
Forties
Ekofisk
Auk
Gordon
SCOTLAND
Edinburgh
Sunderland
Teesside
NORTHERN IRELAND
Belfast
Morecambe
Leeds
Scunthorpe
Easington
Viking
Sheffield
Immingham
Theddlethorpe
REPUBLIC OF IRELAND
Ellesmere Port
ENGLAND
Bacton
Birmingham
Coventry
WALES
Luton
Dagenham
Llanwern
Avonmouth
London
Port Talbot
Swindon
Fawley

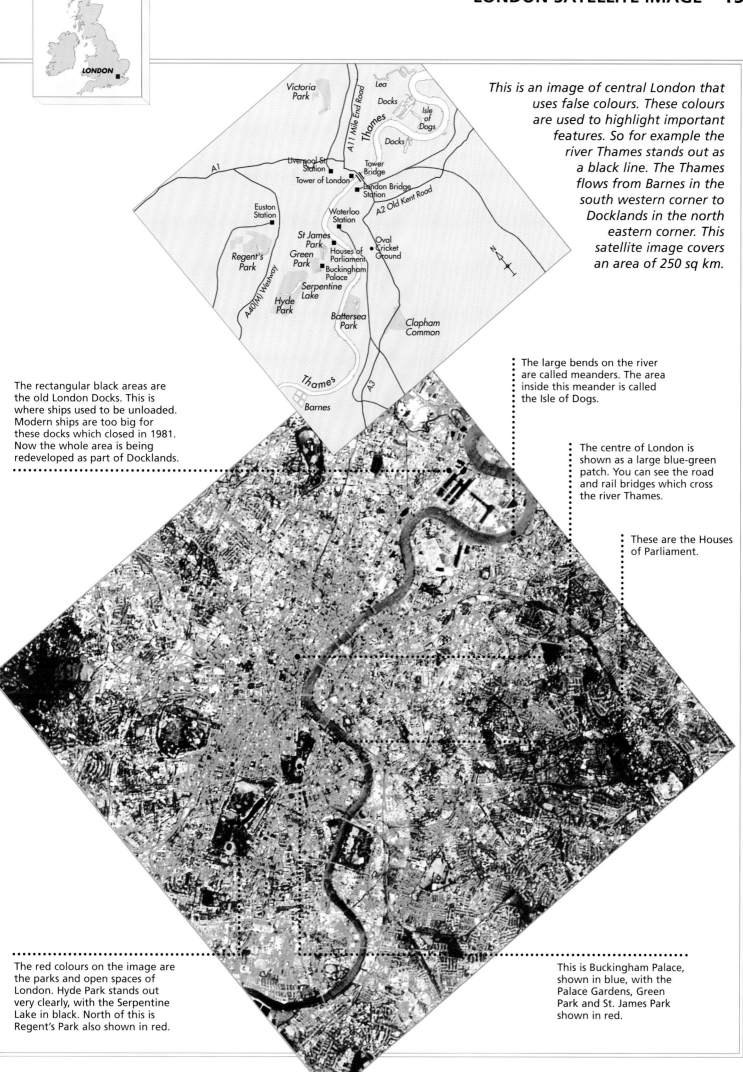

This is an image of central London that uses false colours. These colours are used to highlight important features. So for example the river Thames stands out as a black line. The Thames flows from Barnes in the south western corner to Docklands in the north eastern corner. This satellite image covers an area of 250 sq km.

The large bends on the river are called meanders. The area inside this meander is called the Isle of Dogs.

The centre of London is shown as a large blue-green patch. You can see the road and rail bridges which cross the river Thames.

These are the Houses of Parliament.

The rectangular black areas are the old London Docks. This is where ships used to be unloaded. Modern ships are too big for these docks which closed in 1981. Now the whole area is being redeveloped as part of Docklands.

The red colours on the image are the parks and open spaces of London. Hyde Park stands out very clearly, with the Serpentine Lake in black. North of this is Regent's Park also shown in red.

This is Buckingham Palace, shown in blue, with the Palace Gardens, Green Park and St. James Park shown in red.

KEY

- over 5000 m
- 3000 – 5000 m
- 2000 – 3000 m
- 1000 – 2000 m
- 500 – 1000 m
- 200 – 500 m
- 0 – 200 m
- land below sea level
- Ice cap

▲ 4808 Mountain height (height in metres)

Scale 1 : 20 000 000

0   200   400   600   800 km

Albers Equal Area Conic projection

A. ANDORRA
L. LIECHTENSTEIN
M. MONACO
.M. SAN MARINO

KEY

────	Country boundary
────	Road
────	Railway
········	Ferry route
✈	Airport
■	Capital city
⬤	Large town or city
○	Other town or city

Scale 1 : 20 000 000

0   200   400   600   800 km

Albers Equal Area Conic projection

A. ANDORRA
L. LIECHTENSTEIN
LUX. LUXEMBOURG
M. MONACO
S.M. SAN MARINO

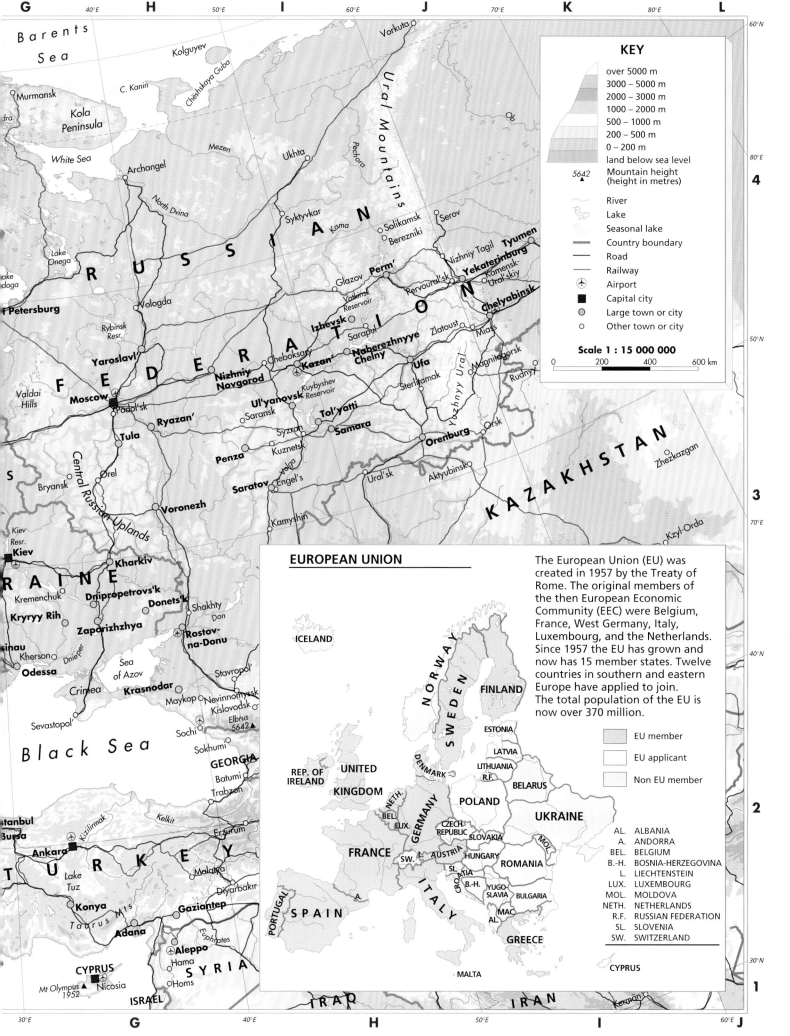

Barents Sea

Murmansk
Kola Peninsula
White Sea
Archangel
North Dvina
Mezen
Ukhta
Vorkuta
Kolguyev
C. Kanin
Cheshskaya Guba

Lake Onega
Lake Ladoga
Petersburg
Vologda
Rybinsk Resr.
Syktyvkar
Kama
Pechora
Solikamsk
Berezniki
Serov
Nizhniy Tagil
Tyumen
Ob

Yaroslavl'
Nizhniy Novgorod
Cheboksary
Glazov
Perm'
Votkinsk Reservoir
Revda'
Yekaterinburg
Nizhniy Tagil
Kamensk-Ural'skiy
Chelyabinsk

Moscow
Podol'sk
Tula
Ryazan'
Saransk
Ul'yanovsk
Izhevsk
Kazan'
Sarapul
Naberezhnyye Chelny
Ufa
Zlatoust
Mias
Magnitogorsk
Rudnyy

Valdai Hills
Orel
Penza
Kuznetsk
Syzran
Kuybyshev Reservoir
Tol'yatti
Samara
Sterlitamak
Yozhnyy Ural

Bryansk
Voronezh
Saratov
Engel's
Kamyshin
Volga
Ural'sk
Aktyubinsk
Orenburg
Orsk

RUSSIAN FEDERATION

KAZAKHSTAN
Zhezkazgan
Kzyl-Orda

Kiev Resr.
Kiev
Kharkiv
Kremenchuk
Dnipropetrovs'k
Donets'k
Shakhty
Don
Kryryy Rih
Zaporizhzhya
Rostov-na-Donu

RAINE
sinau
Kherson
Dnieper
Crimea
Sea of Azov
Stavropol
Krasnodar
Maykop
Nevinnomyssk
Kislovodsk
Elbrus 5642
Odessa
Sevastopol'
Sochi
Sokhumi

Black Sea

Central Russian Uplands

GEORGIA
Batumi
Trabzon

stanbul
Bursa
Ankara
Kizilirmak
Kelkit
Erzurum

TURKEY
Konya
Lake Tuz
Taurus Mts
Malatya
Diyarbakir
Gaziantep
Adana
Euphrates

CYPRUS
Mt Olympus 1952
Nicosia
Aleppo
Hama
Homs
SYRIA
ISRAEL
IRAQ
IRAN
Kerman

Ural Mountains

Yozhnyy Ural

KEY

over 5000 m
3000 – 5000 m
2000 – 3000 m
1000 – 2000 m
500 – 1000 m
200 – 500 m
0 – 200 m
land below sea level
5642 ▲ Mountain height (height in metres)
River
Lake
Seasonal lake
Country boundary
Road
Railway
✈ Airport
■ Capital city
● Large town or city
○ Other town or city

Scale 1 : 15 000 000

0   200   400   600 km

EUROPEAN UNION

The European Union (EU) was created in 1957 by the Treaty of Rome. The original members of the then European Economic Community (EEC) were Belgium, France, West Germany, Italy, Luxembourg, and the Netherlands. Since 1957 the EU has grown and now has 15 member states. Twelve countries in southern and eastern Europe have applied to join. The total population of the EU is now over 370 million.

EU member
EU applicant
Non EU member

ICELAND
NORWAY
SWEDEN
FINLAND
ESTONIA
LATVIA
LITHUANIA
DENMARK
REP. OF IRELAND
UNITED KINGDOM
NETH.
BEL.
LUX.
GERMANY
POLAND
BELARUS
CZECH REPUBLIC
UKRAINE
SLOVAKIA
SW.
AUSTRIA
HUNGARY
MOL.
FRANCE
SL.
CROATIA
ROMANIA
B.-H.
YUGO-SLAVIA
BULGARIA
MAC
ITALY
AL
PORTUGAL
SPAIN
A.
GREECE
MALTA
CYPRUS

AL.   ALBANIA
A.   ANDORRA
BEL. BELGIUM
B.-H. BOSNIA-HERZEGOVINA
L.   LIECHTENSTEIN
LUX. LUXEMBOURG
MOL. MOLDOVA
NETH. NETHERLANDS
R.F. RUSSIAN FEDERATION
SL.   SLOVENIA
SW.   SWITZERLAND

Lambert Azimuthal Equal Area projection

ANNUAL RAINFALL

Heaviest rainfall occurs during autumn and winter when westerly winds blow against the Alps and Apennines. Lowlands in the north and east have less rainfall because they are sheltered. The south has very little rainfall in summer.

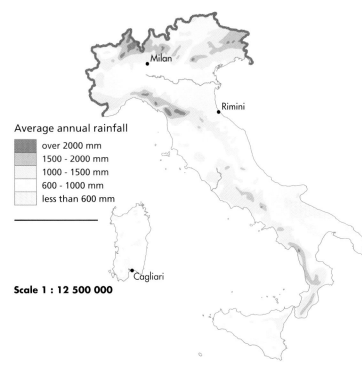

Average annual rainfall

- over 2000 mm
- 1500 - 2000 mm
- 1000 - 1500 mm
- 600 - 1000 mm
- less than 600 mm

Scale 1 : 12 500 000

CLIMATE STATISTICS

The climate of Italy is greatly influenced by relief. The northern and central uplands have lower temperatures. Rainfall is higher to the west of the Apennines than to the east. Winters become milder and summers become hotter and drier as you move further south.

Milan	Jan	Feb	Mar	Apr	May	Jun	Jul	Aug	Sep	Oct	Nov	Dec
Temperature - °C	1	3	8	13	17	21	23	22	19	13	7	2
Rainfall - mm	52	49	65	70	85	89	55	71	72	114	101	80

Rimini	Jan	Feb	Mar	Apr	May	Jun	Jul	Aug	Sep	Oct	Nov	Dec
Temperature - °C	3	6	9	14	18	21	24	24	20	15	9	6
Rainfall - mm	64	36	68	71	57	57	71	61	61	93	114	79

Cagliari	Jan	Feb	Mar	Apr	May	Jun	Jul	Aug	Sep	Oct	Nov	Dec
Temperature - °C	10	10	12	15	19	23	25	25	23	18	14	12
Rainfall - mm	54	54	46	29	25	11	4	7	32	61	79	71

TEMPERATURE: JANUARY

The mountains in the north and the central uplands can have very low temperatures. Northern lowlands are affected by cold winds from Europe. Coastal areas are the warmest.

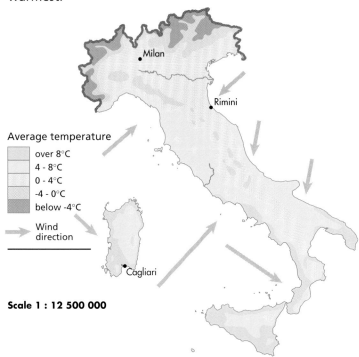

Average temperature

- over 8°C
- 4 - 8°C
- 0 - 4°C
- -4 - 0°C
- below -4°C

→ Wind direction

Scale 1 : 12 500 000

TEMPERATURE: JULY

Sheltered northern lowlands and coastal areas have hot summers. Other areas are cooler due to their altitude. In the south, hot, dry winds from Africa can lead to very high temperatures.

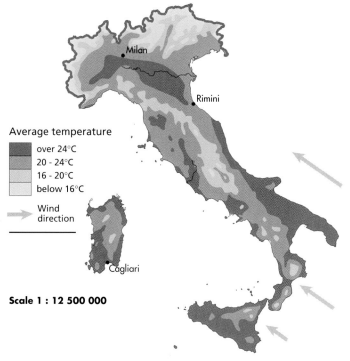

Average temperature

- over 24°C
- 20 - 24°C
- 16 - 20°C
- below 16°C

→ Wind direction

Scale 1 : 12 500 000

National Parks and Protected Areas have been created in Italy to preserve wildlife and natural vegetation. Most of these areas are inland and despite its long coastline, Italy has very few protected coastal areas. Pollution from oil spillage and industrial waste remains around the coast for long periods due to the low tidal movements of the Mediterranean Sea.

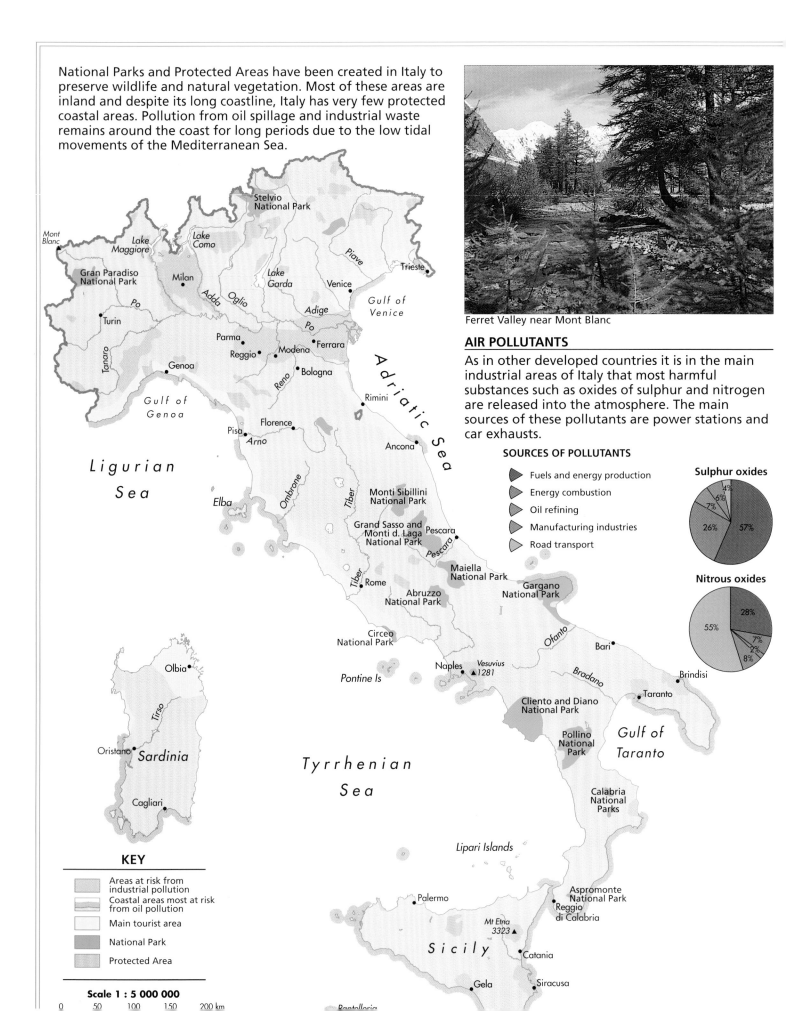

Ferret Valley near Mont Blanc

AIR POLLUTANTS

As in other developed countries it is in the main industrial areas of Italy that most harmful substances such as oxides of sulphur and nitrogen are released into the atmosphere. The main sources of these pollutants are power stations and car exhausts.

SOURCES OF POLLUTANTS

- Fuels and energy production
- Energy combustion
- Oil refining
- Manufacturing industries
- Road transport

Sulphur oxides

57%
26%
7%
6%
4%

Nitrous oxides

28%
55%
8%
2%
7%

Mont Blanc
Lake Maggiore
Lake Como
Stelvio National Park
Piave
Trieste
Gran Paradiso National Park
Milan
Lake Garda
Venice
Gulf of Venice
Adda
Oglio
Adige
Po
Turin
Po
Tanaro
Parma
Reggio
Modena
Ferrara
Genoa
Reno
Bologna
Gulf of Genoa
Rimini
Pisa
Florence
Arno
Ancona
Ombrone
Adriatic Sea

Ligurian Sea

Elba
Tiber
Monti Sibillini National Park
Grand Sasso and Monti d. Laga National Park
Pescara
Pescara
Maiella National Park
Tiber
Rome
Gargano National Park
Abruzzo National Park
Circeo National Park
Ofanto
Bari
Naples
Vesuvius ▲1281
Pontine Is
Bradano
Brindisi
Taranto
Cilento and Diano National Park
Pollino National Park
Gulf of Taranto

Tyrrhenian Sea

Calabria National Parks

Olbia
Tirso
Oristano
Sardinia
Cagliari

Lipari Islands

Palermo
Aspromonte National Park
Reggio di Calabria
Mt Etna 3323 ▲
Sicily
Catania
Gela
Siracusa
Pantelleria

KEY

- Areas at risk from industrial pollution
- Coastal areas most at risk from oil pollution
- Main tourist area
- National Park
- Protected Area

Scale 1 : 5 000 000

0   50   100   150   200 km

This is a simulated natural colour image of Venice and the surrounding area of north east Italy. The image is made of hundreds of tiny frames which were taken at different times of the year. The brown, yellow and green colours of the land area shows how vegetation grew there between the time the first frame was taken and the time the last one was taken. In the same way the colours in the sea to the east of the image show changes in the height and pattern of the waves.

Venice and its lagoon. The city of Venice is the pale grey area.

Sand, mud and silt brought down by rivers like the Adige are deposited in the sea.

Some of the sand, mud and silt is polluted by chemicals from industry and sewage.

Many cities in Europe have pollution problems like Venice.

Sile

Treviso

Padova

Mestre

Venice

Piave

Rovigo

Adige

Venice Lagoon

Gulf of Venice

Tartaro

Po

N

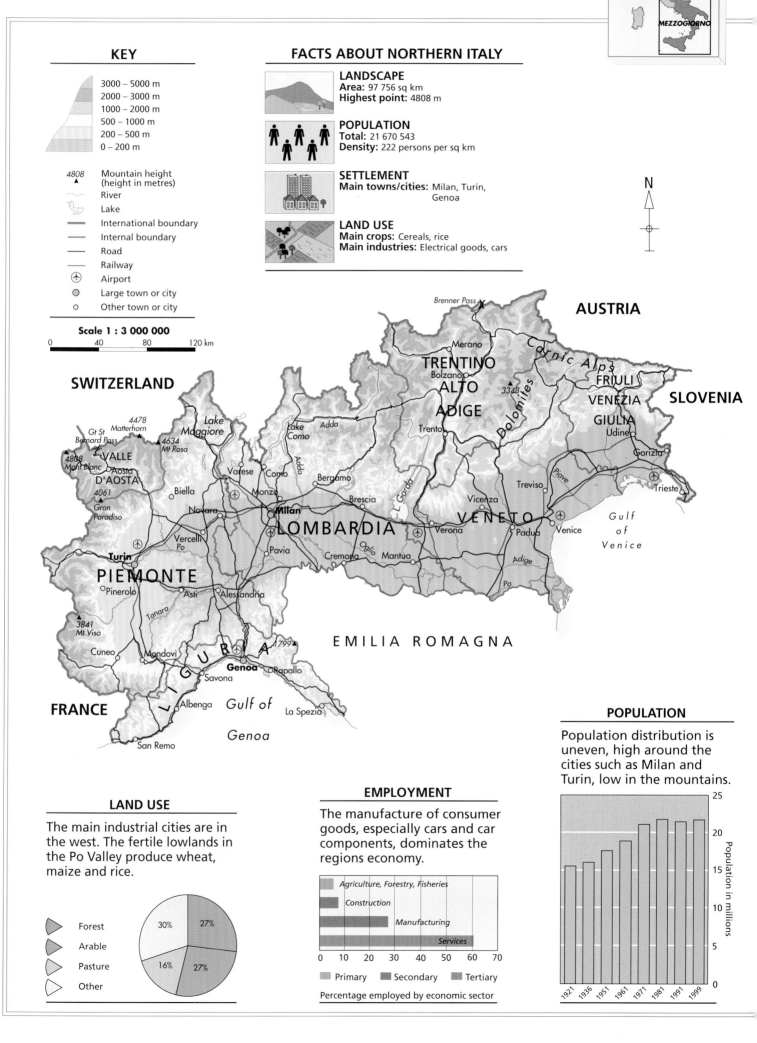

KEY

3000 – 5000 m
2000 – 3000 m
1000 – 2000 m
500 – 1000 m
200 – 500 m
0 – 200 m

▲ 4808   Mountain height (height in metres)
〰 River
  Lake
International boundary
Internal boundary
Road
Railway
⊕ Airport
◎ Large town or city
○ Other town or city

Scale 1 : 3 000 000

0   40   80   120 km

FACTS ABOUT NORTHERN ITALY

LANDSCAPE
Area: 97 756 sq km
Highest point: 4808 m

POPULATION
Total: 21 670 543
Density: 222 persons per sq km

SETTLEMENT
Main towns/cities: Milan, Turin, Genoa

LAND USE
Main crops: Cereals, rice
Main industries: Electrical goods, cars

N

AUSTRIA
SWITZERLAND
SLOVENIA
FRANCE

Brenner Pass

Merano

TRENTINO ALTO ADIGE

Carnic Alps

FRIULI VENEZIA GIULIA

Bolzano

3343 ▲

Dolomites

Trento

Udine

Gorizia

4478 Matterhorn

Lake Maggiore

Lake Como

Adda

Gt St Bernard Pass

4634 Mt Rosa

VALLE D'AOSTA

4808 Mont Blanc

Aosta

4061 Gran Paradiso

Biella

Varese

Como

Adda

Bergamo

Brescia

L. Garda

Piave

Treviso

Trieste 2061

Gulf of Venice

Monza

Novara

Vercelli

Po

Milan

LOMBARDIA

Pavia

Cremona

Oglio

Mantua

Vicenza

Verona

VENETO

Padua

Venice

Turin

PIEMONTE

Pinerolo

Asti

Alessandria

Adige

Po

3841 Mt Viso

Cuneo

Mondovì

LIGURIA

Tanaro

1799 ▲

EMILIA ROMAGNA

Genoa

Rapallo

Savona

Albenga

La Spezia

Gulf of Genoa

San Remo

LAND USE

The main industrial cities are in the west. The fertile lowlands in the Po Valley produce wheat, maize and rice.

◁ Forest
◁ Arable
◁ Pasture
▷ Other

30% | 27%
16% | 27%

EMPLOYMENT

The manufacture of consumer goods, especially cars and car components, dominates the regions economy.

Agriculture, Forestry, Fisheries
Construction
Manufacturing
Services

0   10   20   30   40   50   60   70

■ Primary   ■ Secondary   ■ Tertiary

Percentage employed by economic sector

POPULATION

Population distribution is uneven, high around the cities such as Milan and Turin, low in the mountains.

Population in millions

25
20
15
10
5
0

1921 1936 1951 1961 1971 1981 1991 1999

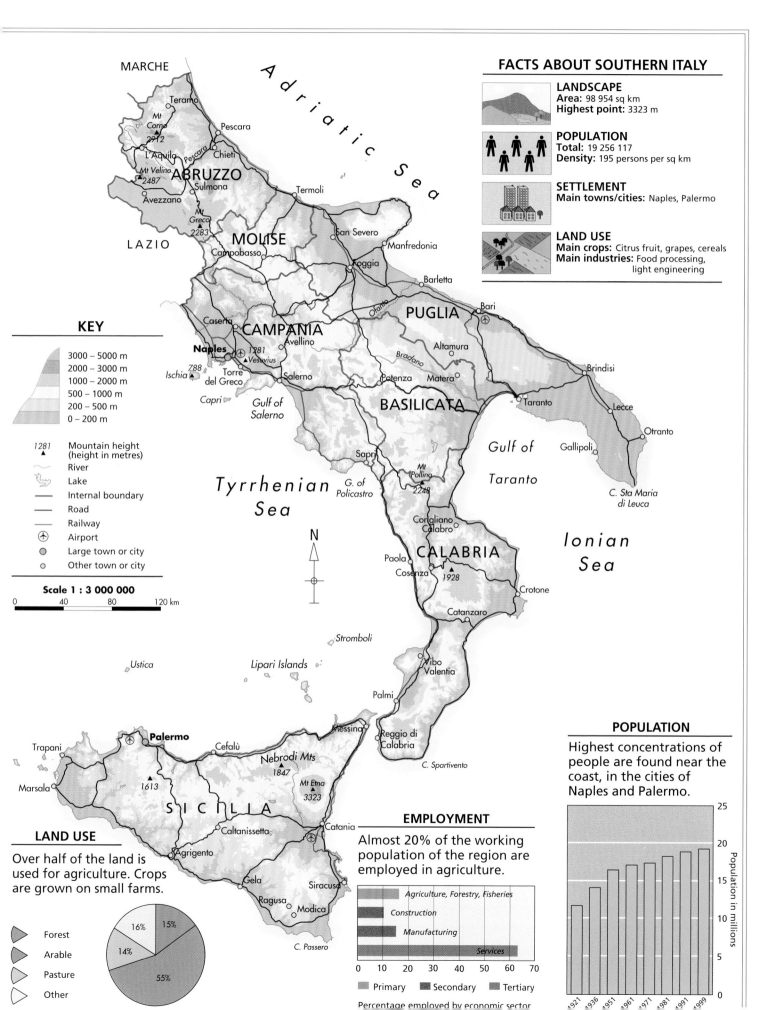

FACTS ABOUT SOUTHERN ITALY

LANDSCAPE
Area: 98 954 sq km
Highest point: 3323 m

POPULATION
Total: 19 256 117
Density: 195 persons per sq km

SETTLEMENT
Main towns/cities: Naples, Palermo

LAND USE
Main crops: Citrus fruit, grapes, cereals
Main industries: Food processing, light engineering

KEY

3000 – 5000 m
2000 – 3000 m
1000 – 2000 m
500 – 1000 m
200 – 500 m
0 – 200 m

1281 ▲ Mountain height (height in metres)
〰 River
Lake
── Internal boundary
── Road
── Railway
⊕ Airport
◉ Large town or city
○ Other town or city

Scale 1 : 3 000 000
0   40   80   120 km

N

LAND USE

Over half of the land is used for agriculture. Crops are grown on small farms.

- Forest
- Arable
- Pasture
- Other

15%
16%
14%
55%

EMPLOYMENT

Almost 20% of the working population of the region are employed in agriculture.

Agriculture, Forestry, Fisheries
Construction
Manufacturing
Services

0   10   20   30   40   50   60   70

■ Primary   ■ Secondary   ■ Tertiary
Percentage employed by economic sector

POPULATION

Highest concentrations of people are found near the coast, in the cities of Naples and Palermo.

Population in millions
25
20
15
10
5
0

1921 1936 1951 1961 1971 1981 1991 1999

Map labels: MARCHE, Teramo, Mt Corno 2912, Pescara, L'Aquila, Chieti, Mt Velino 2487, ABRUZZO, Sulmona, Avezzano, Mt Greco 2283, LAZIO, MOLISE, Campobasso, Termoli, San Severo, Manfredonia, Foggia, Barletta, Bari, PUGLIA, Caserta, CAMPANIA, Avellino, Altamura, Naples, 1281 Vesuvius, Ischia 788, Torre del Greco, Salerno, Bradano, Brindisi, Capri, Gulf of Salerno, Potenza, Matera, BASILICATA, Taranto, Lecce, Sapri, Otranto, Gallipoli, Tyrrhenian Sea, G. of Policastro, Mt Pollino 2248, Gulf of Taranto, C. Sta Maria di Leuca, Ionian Sea, Corigliano Calabro, Paola, CALABRIA, Cosenza 1928, Crotone, Catanzaro, Stromboli, Vibo Valentia, Lipari Islands, Ustica, Palmi, Messina, Reggio di Calabria, C. Spartivento, Palermo, Trapani, Cefalù, Nebrodi Mts 1847, 1613, SICILIA, Mt Etna 3323, Marsala, Caltanissetta, Catania, Agrigento, Gela, Siracusa, Ragusa, Modica, C. Passero, Adriatic Sea, Pescara (river), Ofanto

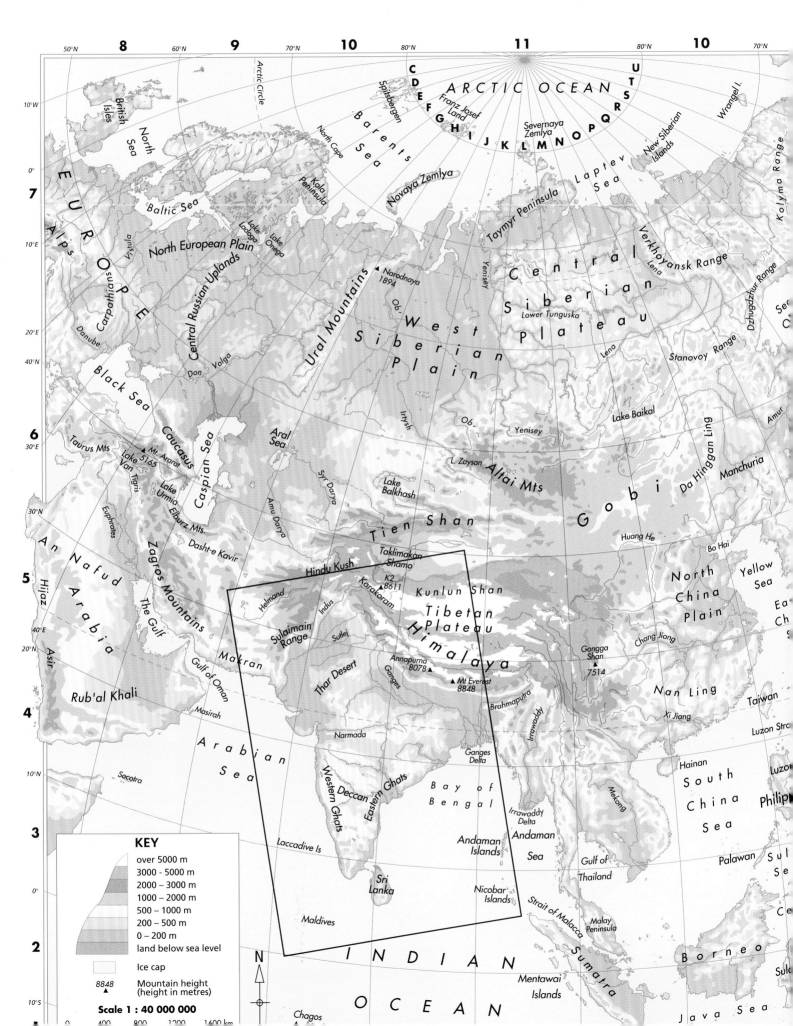

KEY

over 5000 m
3000 – 5000 m
2000 – 3000 m
1000 – 2000 m
500 – 1000 m
200 – 500 m
0 – 200 m
land below sea level

Ice cap

▲ 8848   Mountain height
(height in metres)

Scale 1 : 40 000 000

0   400   800   1200   1600 km

ARCTIC OCEAN

C
D
E
F
G
H
I
J
K
L
M
N
O
P
Q
R
S
T
U

British Isles
North Sea
Baltic Sea
Barents Sea
Spitsbergen
Franz Josef Land
Severnaya Zemlya
Novaya Zemlya
North Cape
Kola Peninsula
Lake Ladoga
Lake Onega
Taymyr Peninsula
Laptev Sea
New Siberian Islands
Wrangel I.
Kolyma Range

EUROPE
Alps
Carpathians
Vistula
Danube
Black Sea
North European Plain
Central Russian Uplands
Don
Volga
Ural Mountains
▲ Narodnaya 1894
Ob'
West Siberian Plain
Irtysh
Ob'
Yenisey
Yenisey
Central Siberian Plateau
Lower Tunguska
Lena
Lena
Verkhoyansk Range
Stanovoy Range
Dzhugdzhur Range
Sea

Taurus Mts
Caucasus
▲ Mt Ararat 5165
Lake Van
Lake Urmia
Tigris
Euphrates
Elburz Mts.
Caspian Sea
Zagros Mountains
Dasht-e Kavir
Aral Sea
Syr Darya
Amu Darya
Lake Balkhash
L. Zaysan
Altai Mts
Lake Baikal
Da Hinggan Ling
Manchuria
Amur

An Nafud
Hijaz
Arabia
The Gulf
Gulf of Oman
Makran
Hindu Kush
Taklimakan Shamo
Karakoram ▲ 8611
K2
Kunlun Shan
Tien Shan
Tibetan Plateau
Gobi
Huang He
Bo Hai
North China Plain
Yellow Sea

Asir
Rub'al Khali
Masirah
Sulaimain Range
Helmand
Indus
Sutlej
Thar Desert
Ganges
Annapurna 8078 ▲
Himalaya
▲ Mt Everest 8848
Brahmaputra
Gongga Shan 7514
Chang Jiang
Nan Ling
Xi Jiang
Taiwan
Luzon Stra

Arabian Sea
Socotra
Narmada
Western Ghats
Deccan
Eastern Ghats
Bay of Bengal
Ganges Delta
Irrawaddy
Irrawaddy Delta
Andaman
Andaman Sea
Mekong
Gulf of Thailand
Hainan
South China Sea
Luzo
Palawan
Sul
Philip

Laccadive Is
Sri Lanka
Maldives
Andaman Islands
Nicobar Islands
Strait of Malacca
Malay Peninsula
Sumatra
Borneo
Sula

N

INDIAN OCEAN

Mentawai Islands
Chagos
Java Sea

8   9   10   11   10

50°N   60°N   70°N   80°N   80°N   70°N
Arctic Circle
10°W
0°
7
10°E
6
20°E
40°N
30°E
30°N
5
40°E
20°N
4
10°N
3
0°
2
10°S

8

60°N

160°W

170°W

180°

40°N

170°E

30°N

160°E

Tropic of Cancer

20°N

10°N

Equator 0°

10°S

130°E **P** 140°E **Q** 150°E

PACIFIC

OCEAN

Bering Sea

Aleutian Islands

Kuril Islands

kkaido

Saipan

Guam

Yap

Caroline Islands

Palau

nao

Halmahera

Misoöl

ula Is

Seram

New Guinea

Puncak Jaya 5030

Bismarck Sea

New Britain

Timor Sea

Gulf of Carpentaria

C. York

Coral Sea

Lambert Azimuthal Equal Area projection

The red box on the map opposite shows the area of the image below.

The valley of the river Indus in Pakistan stands out on this image as a dark brown area.

The snow covered Himalayan Mountains stand out clearly in northern India.

Sri Lanka is the large island off the southeastern coast of India. The bright colours show that it is mountainous especially in the southwestern part of the island.

The river Ganges enters the sea in the Bay of Bengal. The river can be seen as a thin blue line. Where the river enters the sea a large delta has formed.

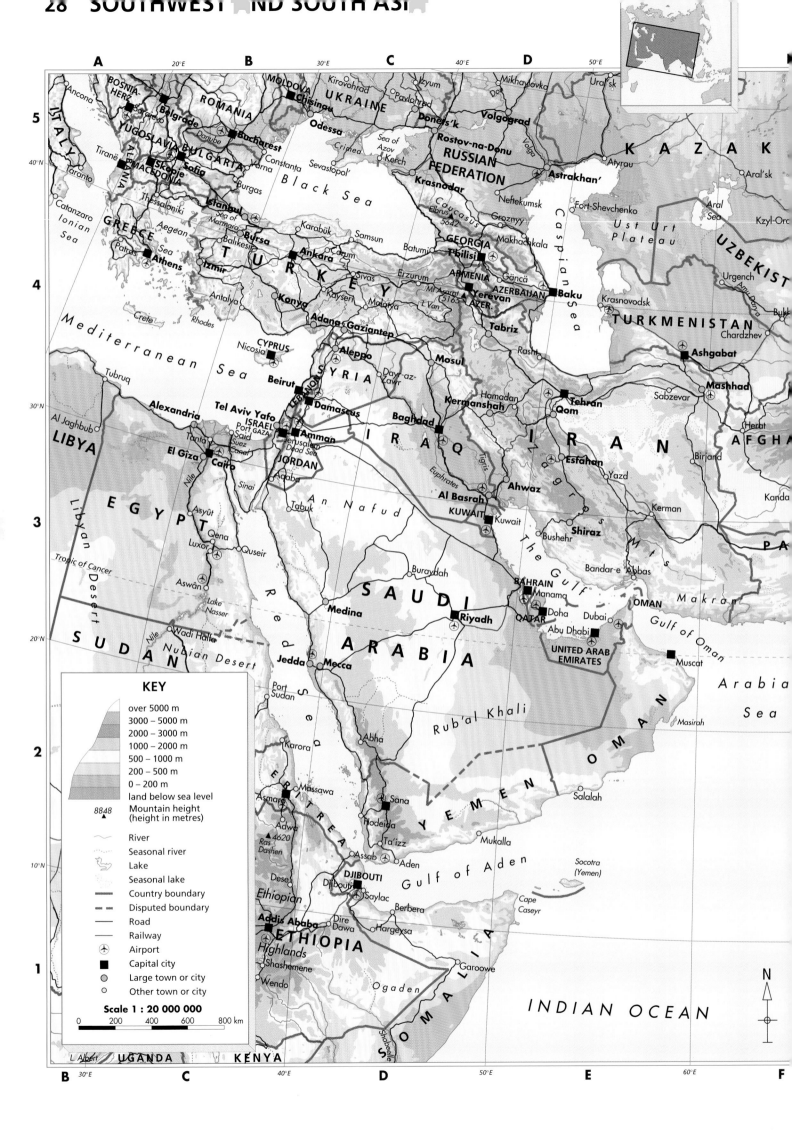

KEY

over 5000 m
3000 – 5000 m
2000 – 3000 m
1000 – 2000 m
500 – 1000 m
200 – 500 m
0 – 200 m
land below sea level

8848 ▲ Mountain height
(height in metres)

〜〜 River
.... Seasonal river
Lake
Seasonal lake
――― Country boundary
- - - Disputed boundary
――― Road
――― Railway
✈ Airport
■ Capital city
● Large town or city
○ Other town or city

Scale 1 : 20 000 000

0   200   400   600   800 km

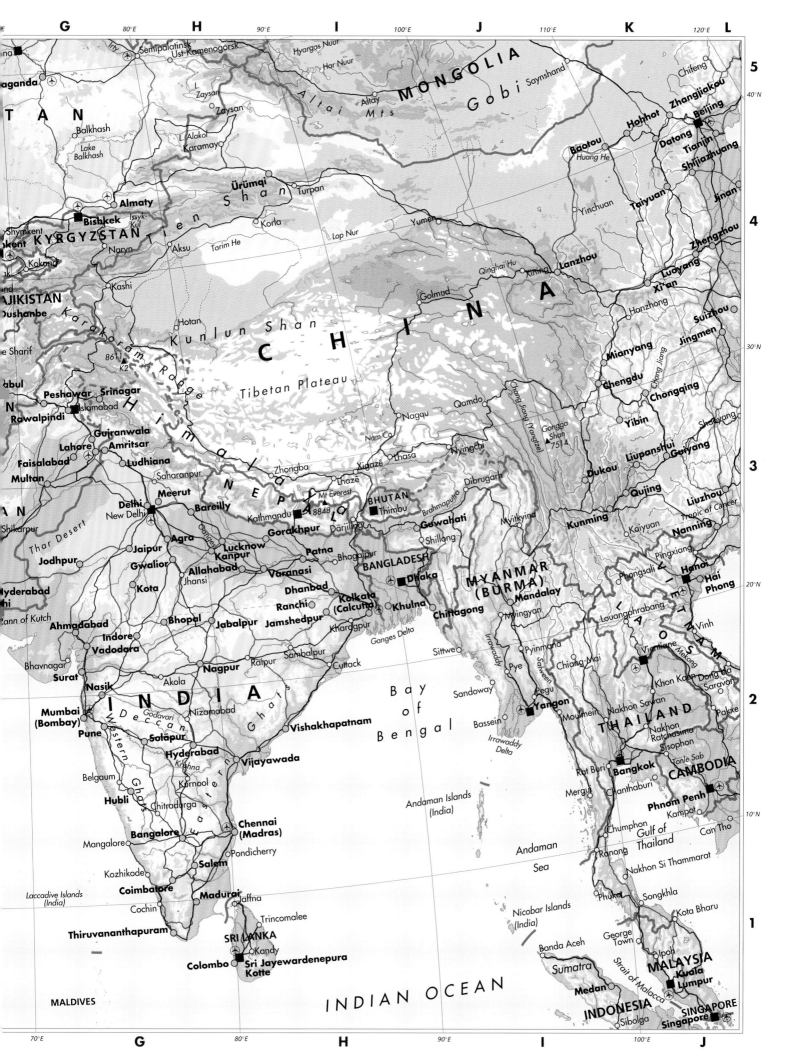

Lambert Azimuthal Equal Area projection

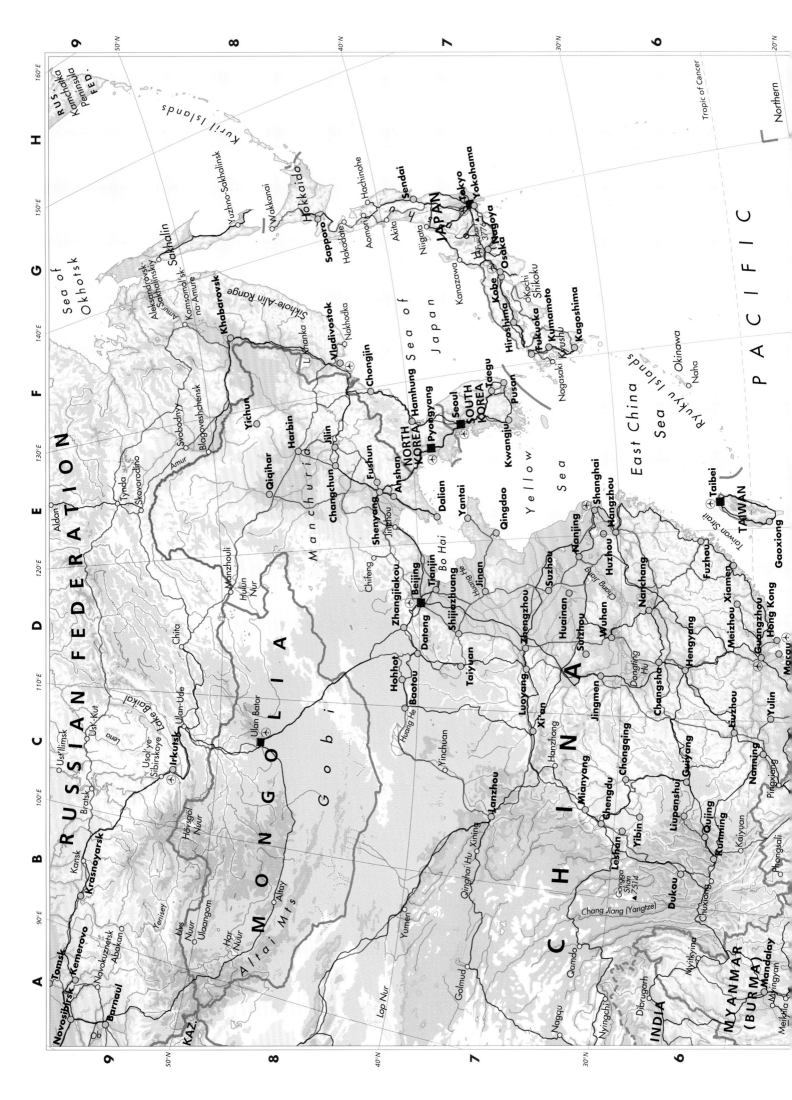

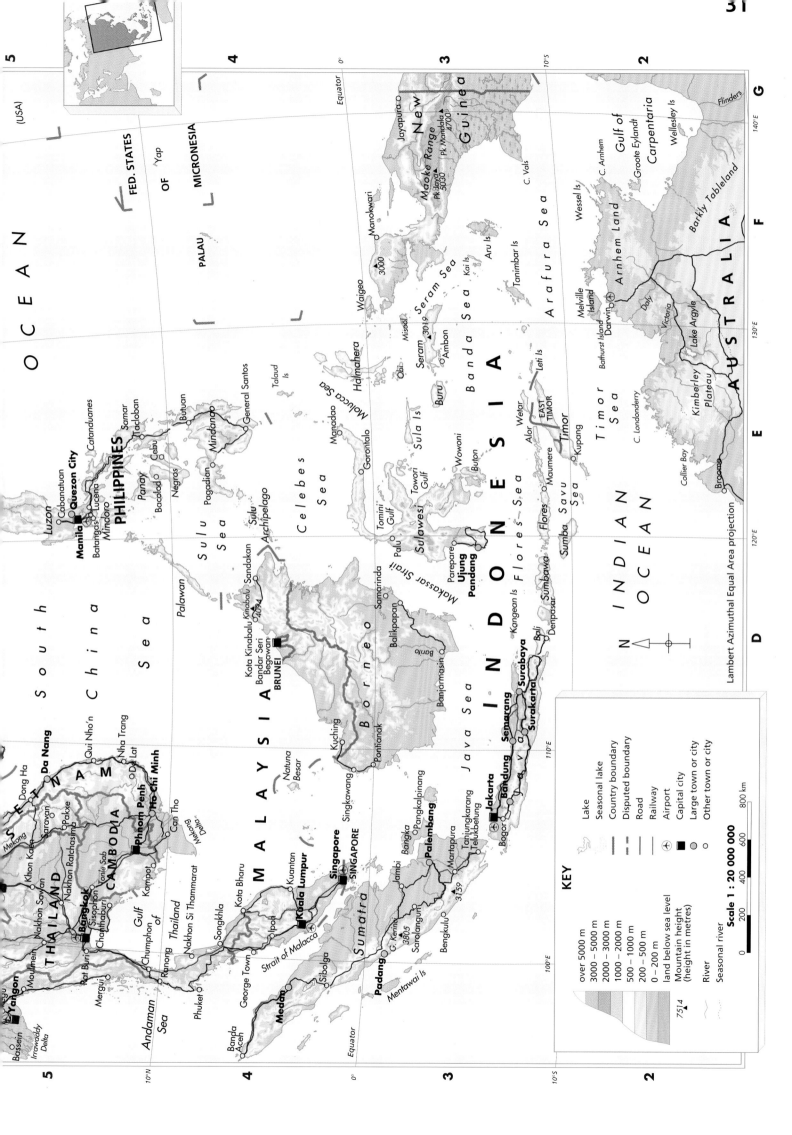

FACTS ABOUT JAPAN

LANDSCAPE
Area: 378 000 sq km
Highest point: 3776 m

POPULATION
Total: 126 876 000
Density: 336 persons per sq km

SETTLEMENT
% Urban population: 78
Main towns/cities: Tokyo, Yokohama, Osaka, Nagoya

LAND USE
Main crops: Rice, potatoes, sugar cane
Main industries: Motor vehicles, steel, machinery, electrical equipment, chemicals

DEVELOPMENT INDICATORS
Life expectancy: male 77, female 84
GNP per capita: US$ 32 350
Primary school enrolment ratio: 102
% Access to safe water: 97

CHINA

RUSSIAN FEDERATION

Sikhote-Alin Range

La Pérouse Strait

Wakkanai

Sea of Okhotsk

Monbetsu

Asahikawa
Kitami

Asahi-dake 2290
Hokkaido

Otaru
Sapporo
Yubari
Obihiro
Kushiro

Ishikari
Hidaka-sammyaku

Tomakomai
Muroran
Samani

Mori
Hakodate

Tsugaru-kaikyo

To Nakhodka

PACIFIC

Goshogawara
Aomori
Hachinohe

Hirosaki
Noshiro
Odate

OCEAN

Akita

Morioka
Miyako

Kamaishi
Sakata
Ichinoseki

Omono

Yamagata
Ishinomaki

Sadoga-shima
Niigata
Sendai
Fukushima
Aizu-wakamatsu
Koriyama
Iwaki

Agano
Nagaoka

Toyama-wan

Kashiwazaki

Hitachi
Joetsu
Takaoka
JAPAN
Utsunomiya
Kanazawa
Toyama
Nagano
Maebashi
Komatsu
Yariga-take
Oyama
Mito
3180
Ueda
Tsuchiura
Fukui
Matsumoto
Kofu
Sakura
Tenryu
Tokyo
Chiba

SOUTH KOREA

Kangnŭng

Tok-to (Take-shima)

Oki-shoto

Ulsan
Pusan

Tsushima

Matsue
Tottori

Chugoku-sanchi

Maizuru

Ogaki Gifu
Ichinomiya Fuji-san
Yokohama Kawasaki
Ichinomiya
Toyota
3776
Yokosuka
Biwa-ko
Numazu
Kyoto
Nagoya
Shizuoka
Okayama
Kobe
Suzuka
Hiroshima
Sakai
Osaka
Tsu
Hamamatsu

Higashi-suido
Shimonoseki
Matsusaka
Kita-Kyushu
Takamatsu
Ise
Iki-shima
Seto-
Matsuyama
nai kai
Wakayama
1981
Shikoku-sanchi
1955
Fukuoka
Shikoku
Sasebo
Kurume
1229
Nagasaki
Kochi
Tokushima
1788
Izu-shoto
Kumamoto
1759
Hachijo-jima
1739
Kyushu
1700
Miyazaki
Kagoshima

Osumi-kaikyo

Tanega-shima

Yaku-shima

Tokara-retto

KEY

3000 – 5000 m	Country boundary
2000 – 3000 m	Road
1000 – 2000 m	Railway
500 – 1000 m	Ferry route
200 – 500 m	Airport
0 – 200 m	Capital city
3776 ▲ Mountain height (height in metres)	Large town or city
River	Other town or city
Lake	

Japanese name forms

-dake	peak
-hanto	peninsula
-jima	island
-kai	bay, inlet
-kaikyo	strait
-ko	lake
-nada	sea, gulf
-retto	chain of islands
-san	mountain
-sanchi	mountainous area
-shima	island
-suido	strait, channel
-to	island
-wan	sea
-yama	mountain

Scale 1 : 7 500 000

0   75   150   225   300 km

Albers Equal Area Conic projection

ANNUAL RAINFALL

The driest parts of Japan are in the north, on the island of Hokkaido. Most rain falls on the high mountain tops and the southern and western coasts.

Average annual rainfall

- over 3000 mm
- 2000 - 3000 mm
- 1500 - 2000 mm
- 1000 - 1500 mm
- less than 1000 mm

Scale 1 : 15 000 000

CLIMATE STATISTICS

The table below lists average monthly temperature in degrees centigrade and average monthly rainfall in millimetres for three weather stations in Japan.

Sapporo	Jan	Feb	Mar	Apr	May	Jun	Jul	Aug	Sep	Oct	Nov	Dec
Temperature - °C	-5	-4	0	6	12	16	20	21	17	11	4	-2
Rainfall - mm	114	92	78	65	59	76	80	131	142	115	104	101

Tokyo	Jan	Feb	Mar	Apr	May	Jun	Jul	Aug	Sep	Oct	Nov	Dec
Temperature - °C	5	5	8	14	18	22	25	27	23	17	12	7
Rainfall - mm	54	63	102	128	148	181	125	137	193	181	93	56

Kagoshima	Jan	Feb	Mar	Apr	May	Jun	Jul	Aug	Sep	Oct	Nov	Dec
Temperature - °C	7	8	11	16	20	23	27	28	25	20	14	9
Rainfall - mm	95	106	147	256	275	475	323	209	211	108	92	80

TEMPERATURE: JANUARY

In January temperatures fall below 0°C in the north of Japan. On the south coast and on the southern island of Kyushu the winter is much milder.

Average temperature

- 4 - 8°C
- 0 - 4°C
- -8 - 0°C
- below -8°C
- → Wind direction

Scale 1 : 15 000 000

TEMPERATURE: AUGUST

Most of Japan is very warm during the summer, especially in the southern part of the country. Temperatures are cooler on the high mountains in the north.

Average temperature

- over 26°C
- 22 - 26°C
- 18 - 22°C
- below 18°C
- → Wind direction

Scale 1 : 15 000 000

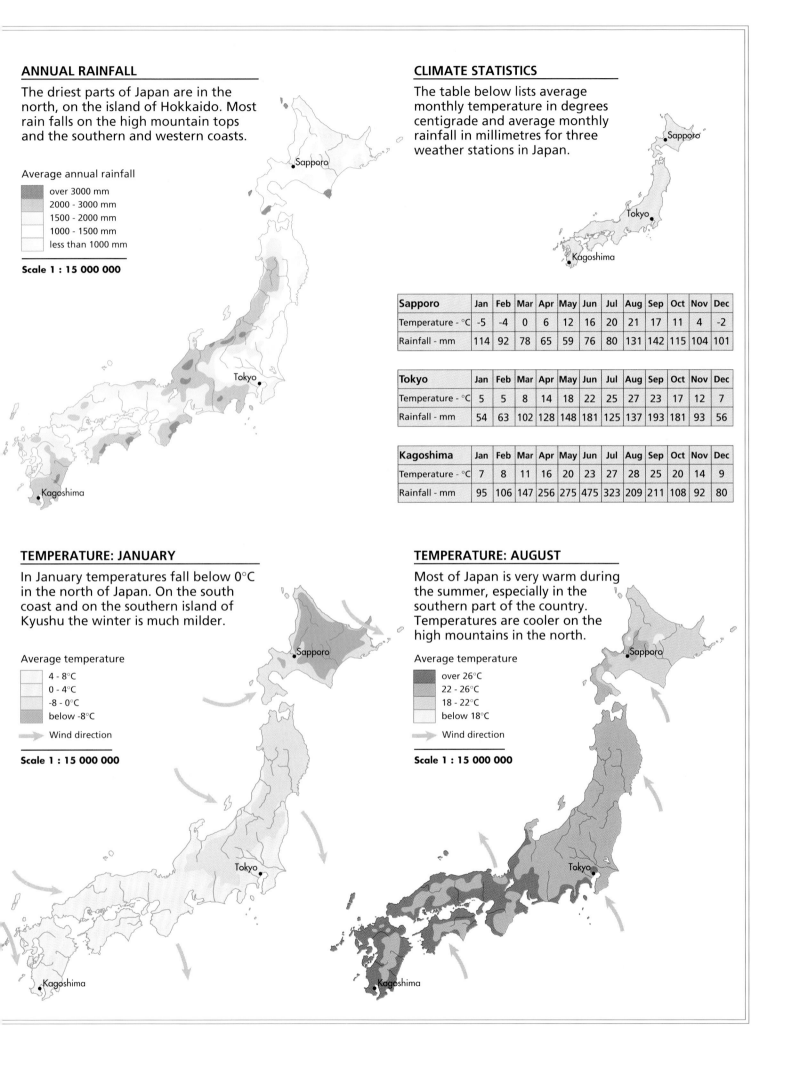

Japan is situated on the 'Ring of Fire' around the Pacific Ocean. There are almost 200 volcanoes in the 'Ring of Fire' and over 20 are still active. Earthquakes are more disastrous than volcanic eruptions in Japan where 5000 earthquakes are recorded annually. The main earthquake zones lie on the Pacific side of Japan. Strong earthquakes may destroy roads and railways, collapse houses and result in many casualties.

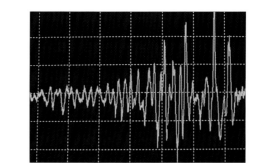

Earthquake seismograph :
A seismograph is used to record the horizontal or vertical vibration caused during the course of an earthquake. The vertical divisions represent time intervals of 5 seconds.

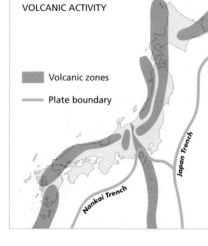

VOLCANIC ACTIVITY

- Volcanic zones
- Plate boundary

Japan Trench

Nankai Trench

Kobe Earthquake :
In 1995 Kobe was struck by a huge earthquake which measured 7.1 on the Richter scale. The centre of the quake was close to the city, caused extensive damage and killed over 5000 people.

Tokachi

Hokkaido

Sapporo

Usu

Komaga-take

Chokai

Zao

Honshu

Yake-Dake

Tokyo

Nagoya

Fuji

Kobe

Shikoku

Fuji :
Situated on the island of Honshu, Fuji is a dormant volcano which has not erupted since 1707. At 3776 m, it is the highest mountain in Japan and has a crater which is 610 metres in diameter.

Unzen *Aso*

Kyushu

Kagoshima *Kirishima*

Sakurajima

KEY

- Volcanic rocks
- ▲ Active volcano (erupted since 1850)
- △ Other volcano
- ● Major earthquake

Scale 1 : 9 000 000

RICHTER SCALE

The scale of measurement used to describe the strength of an earthquake is known as the Richter Scale. The scale measures the energy which is released at the centre of an earthquake. Every year about 50 000 quakes measuring 3 - 4 are recorded worldwide, while only 800 measuring 5 - 6 occur.

9	Over 8.0 most powerful earthquake
8	7.0 - 8.0 major earthquake
7	6.0 - 7.0 destructive earthquake
6	
5	4.5 - 6.0 earthquake causes local damage
4	3.5 - 4.5 earthquake felt by many people
3	2.5 - 3.5 earthquake recorded but not felt
2	
1	below 2.5 earthquake not recorded
0	

Sakurajima :
Sakurajima is an active volcano situated in Kagoshima Bay. Its eruptions are generally gentle with little explosive activity.

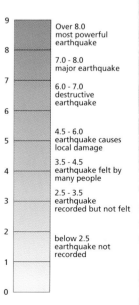

This image of Sakurajima volcano was taken by a Landsat satellite. The image uses false colours to highlight the contrasts in the different ways in which the land is used. Black is used to show those parts of the image which are sea. Towns and urban areas are shown in pink, whilst mountains and forests show up in dark grey-greens.

This image shows the eruption of Sakurajima volcano in Japan. You can see the plume of ash and steam rising from the centre of the volcano.

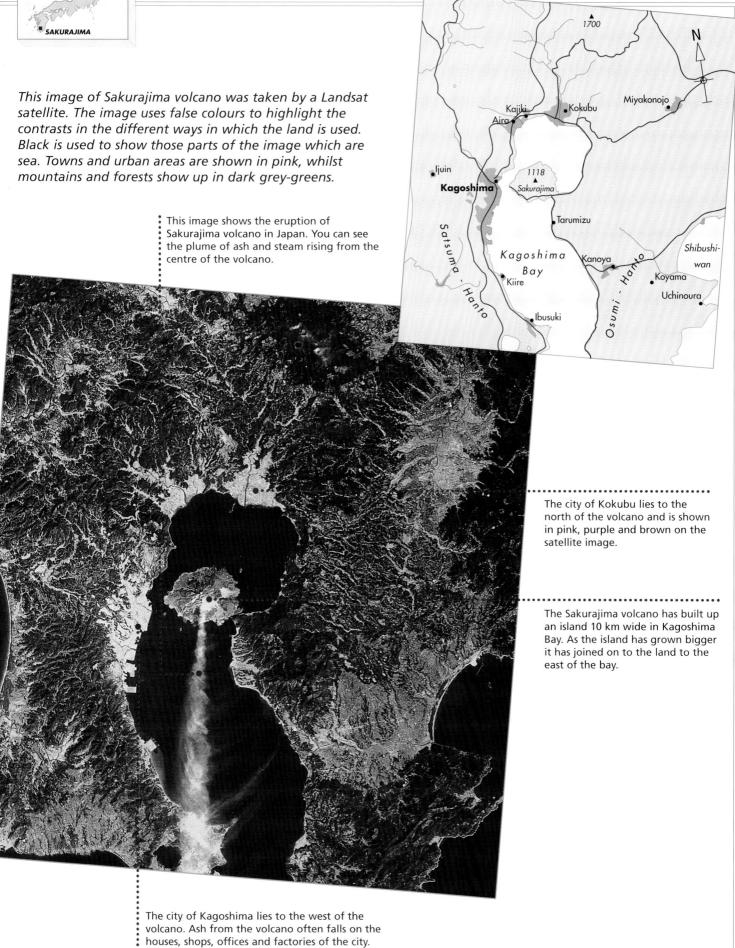

The city of Kokubu lies to the north of the volcano and is shown in pink, purple and brown on the satellite image.

The Sakurajima volcano has built up an island 10 km wide in Kagoshima Bay. As the island has grown bigger it has joined on to the land to the east of the bay.

The city of Kagoshima lies to the west of the volcano. Ash from the volcano often falls on the houses, shops, offices and factories of the city.

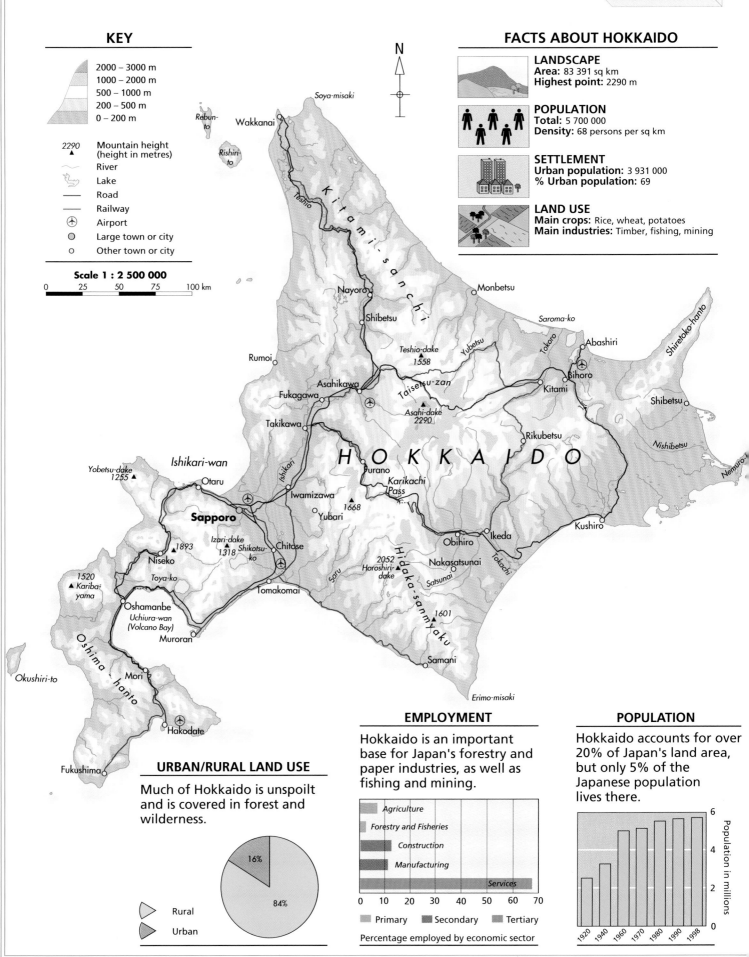

KEY

	2000 – 3000 m
	1000 – 2000 m
	500 – 1000 m
	200 – 500 m
	0 – 200 m

2290 ▲ Mountain height (height in metres)

River

Lake

Road

Railway

⊕ Airport

◉ Large town or city

○ Other town or city

Scale 1 : 2 500 000

0 25 50 75 100 km

N

FACTS ABOUT HOKKAIDO

LANDSCAPE
Area: 83 391 sq km
Highest point: 2290 m

POPULATION
Total: 5 700 000
Density: 68 persons per sq km

SETTLEMENT
Urban population: 3 931 000
% Urban population: 69

LAND USE
Main crops: Rice, wheat, potatoes
Main industries: Timber, fishing, mining

URBAN/RURAL LAND USE

Much of Hokkaido is unspoilt and is covered in forest and wilderness.

16%
84%

▷ Rural
▷ Urban

EMPLOYMENT

Hokkaido is an important base for Japan's forestry and paper industries, as well as fishing and mining.

Agriculture
Forestry and Fisheries
Construction
Manufacturing
Services

0 10 20 30 40 50 60 70

■ Primary ■ Secondary ■ Tertiary

Percentage employed by economic sector

POPULATION

Hokkaido accounts for over 20% of Japan's land area, but only 5% of the Japanese population lives there.

6
4
2
0

Population in millions

1920 1940 1960 1970 1980 1990 1998

Conic Equidistant projecti

FACTS ABOUT KYUSHU

LANDSCAPE
Area: 42 072 sq km
Highest point: 1788 m

POPULATION
Total: 13 462 000
Density: 320 persons per sq km

SETTLEMENT
Urban population: 7 305 000
% Urban population: 50

LAND USE
Main crops: Vegetables, rice
Main industries: Car manufacturing, electronics, steel production

KEY

	1000 – 2000 m
	500 – 1000 m
	200 – 500 m
	0 – 200 m
1788 ▲	Mountain height (height in metres)
	River
	Lake
	Road
	Railway
✈	Airport
⊙	Large town or city
○	Other town or city

Scale 1 : 2 500 000

0   25   50   75   100 km

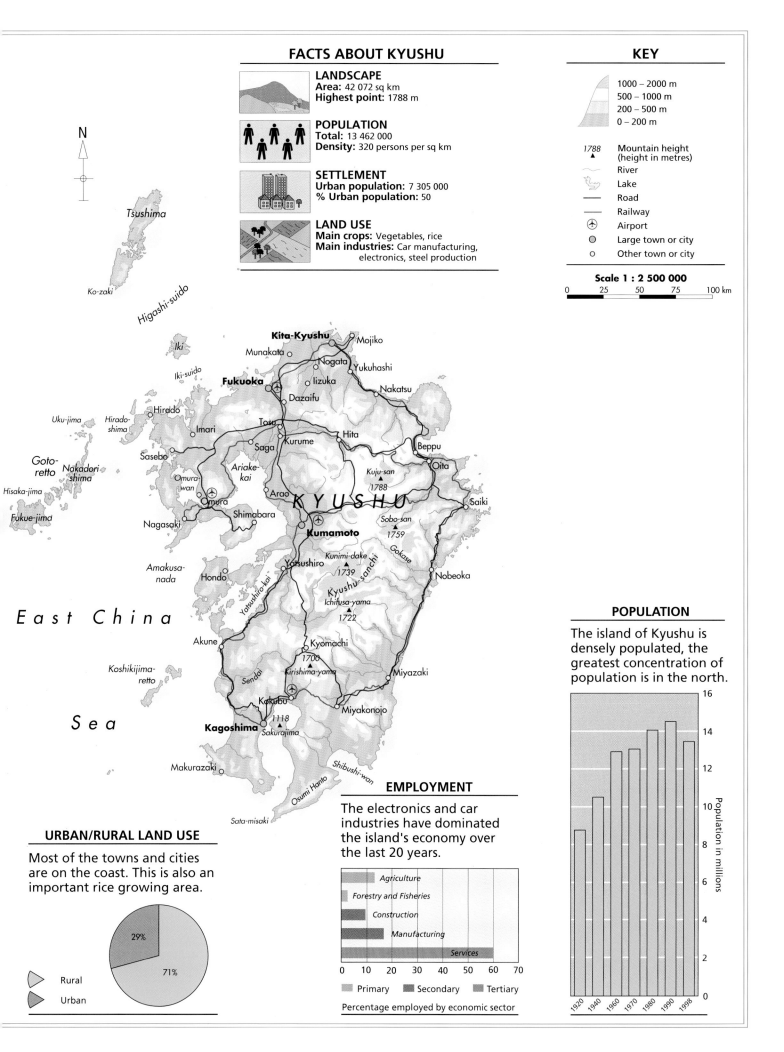

POPULATION

The island of Kyushu is densely populated, the greatest concentration of population is in the north.

EMPLOYMENT

The electronics and car industries have dominated the island's economy over the last 20 years.

Agriculture
Forestry and Fisheries
Construction
Manufacturing
Services

0   10   20   30   40   50   60   70

Primary   Secondary   Tertiary

Percentage employed by economic sector

URBAN/RURAL LAND USE

Most of the towns and cities are on the coast. This is also an important rice growing area.

29%
71%

Rural
Urban

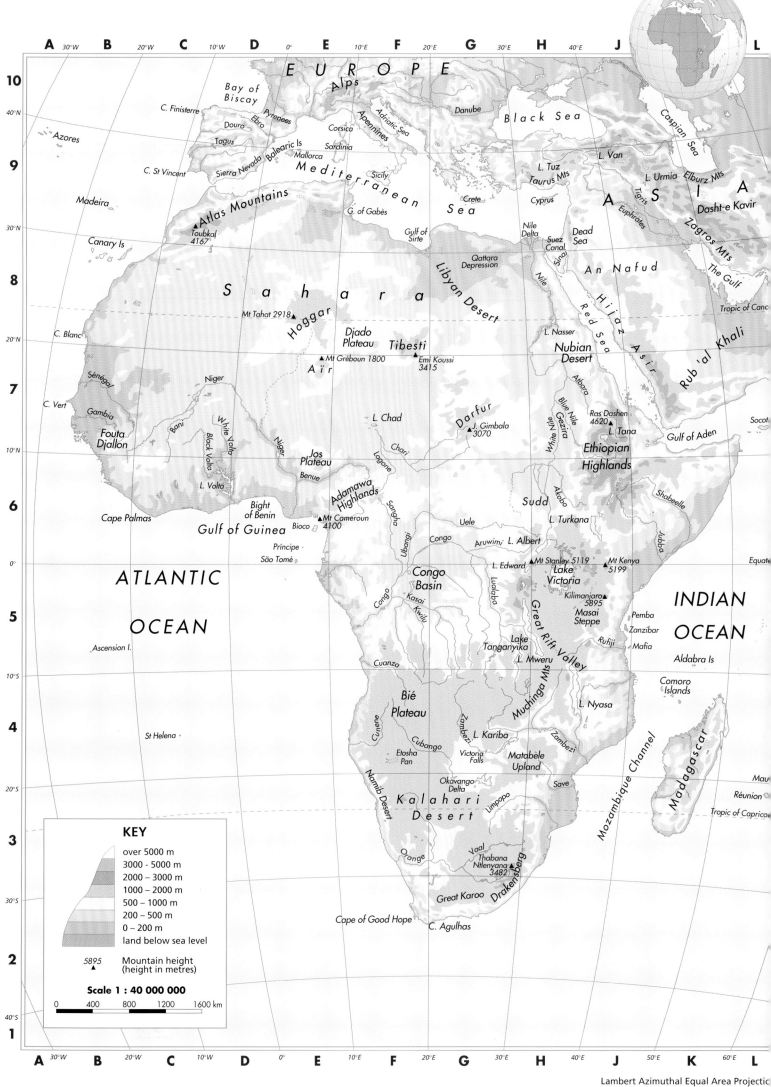

KEY

- over 5000 m
- 3000 - 5000 m
- 2000 - 3000 m
- 1000 - 2000 m
- 500 - 1000 m
- 200 - 500 m
- 0 - 200 m
- land below sea level

▲ 5895 Mountain height (height in metres)

Scale 1 : 40 000 000

0   400   800   1200   1600 km

Lambert Azimuthal Equal Area Projection

This is an infra-red satellite image of the delta of the river Nile, the Sinai peninsula and the neighbouring parts of Israel, Jordan and Saudi Arabia. Most of this area is desert and this is shown in the pale pinky-brown colour. The red colour in the delta of the river Nile shows that most of the land here is used for farming. The pale blue areas on the edge of the delta are shallow lagoons.

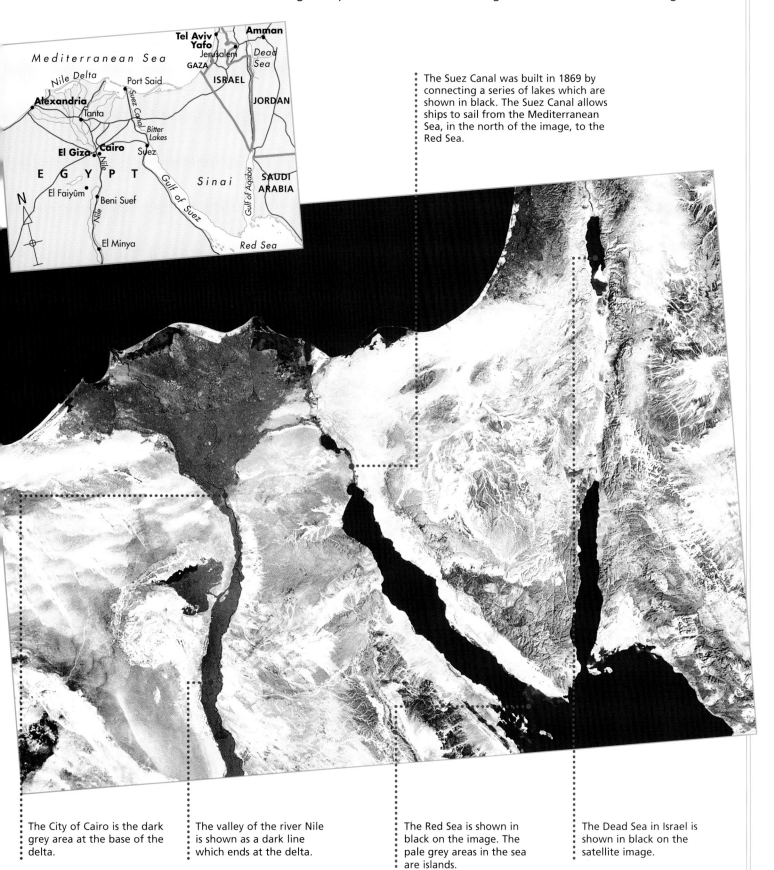

The Suez Canal was built in 1869 by connecting a series of lakes which are shown in black. The Suez Canal allows ships to sail from the Mediterranean Sea, in the north of the image, to the Red Sea.

The City of Cairo is the dark grey area at the base of the delta.

The valley of the river Nile is shown as a dark line which ends at the delta.

The Red Sea is shown in black on the image. The pale grey areas in the sea are islands.

The Dead Sea in Israel is shown in black on the satellite image.

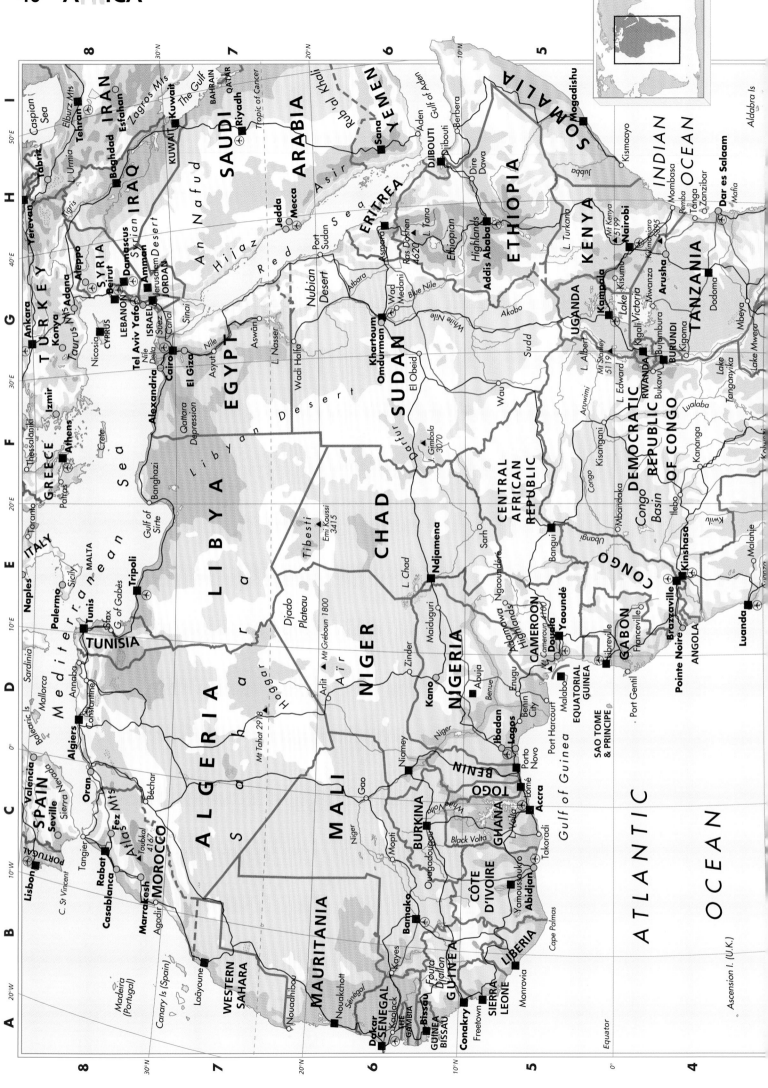

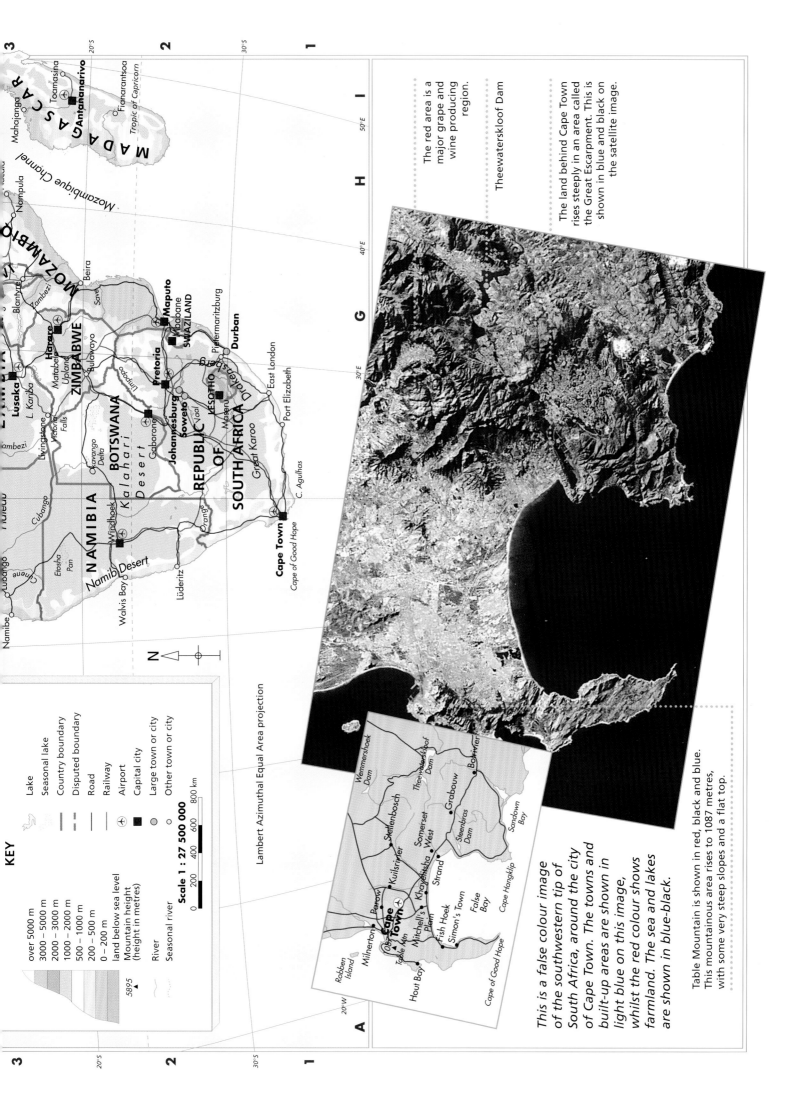

KEY

over 5000 m
3000 – 5000 m
2000 – 3000 m
1000 – 2000 m
500 – 1000 m
200 – 500 m
0 – 200 m
land below sea level

Mountain height
(height in metres)

▲ 5895

River

Seasonal river

Lake

Seasonal lake

Country boundary

Disputed boundary

Road

Railway

✈ Airport

■ Capital city

● Large town or city

○ Other town or city

Scale 1 : 27 500 000

0   200   400   600   800 km

Lambert Azimuthal Equal Area projection

N

This is a false colour image of the southwestern tip of South Africa, around the city of Cape Town. The towns and built-up areas are shown in light blue on this image, whilst the red colour shows farmland. The sea and lakes are shown in blue-black.

Table Mountain is shown in red, black and blue. This mountainous area rises to 1087 metres, with some very steep slopes and a flat top.

The red area is a major grape and wine producing region.

Theewaterskloof Dam

The land behind Cape Town rises steeply in an area called the Great Escarpment. This is shown in blue and black on the satellite image.

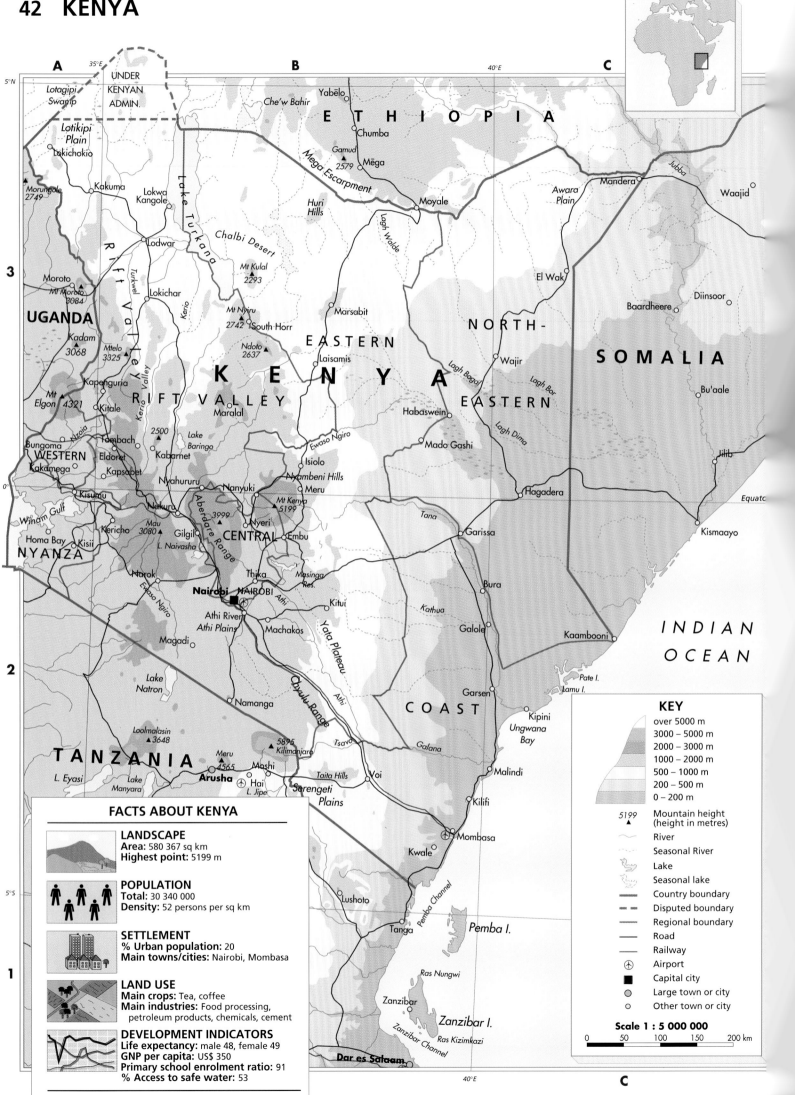

UNDER KENYAN ADMIN.

5°N · 35°E

ETHIOPIA

Lotagipi Swamp
Lotikipi Plain
Lokichokio
Che'w Bahir
Yabēlo
Chumba
Gamud 2579
Mēga
▲ *Morungole* 2749
Kakuma
Lokwa Kangole
Lake Turkana
Huri Hills
Moyale
Mandera
Jubba
Waajid

UGANDA

Moroto
▲ *Mt Moroto* 3084
Lodwar
Lokichar
Mt Kulal 2293
Marsabit
El Wak
Baardheere
Diinsoor

3

Kadam 3068
Mtelo 3325
Kerio
▲ *Mt Nyiru* 2742
South Horr
Ndoto 2637
EASTERN
Laisamis
NORTH-
SOMALIA
Wajir
Lagh Bogal

Mt ▲ *Elgon* 4321
Kapenguria
Kitale
RIFT VALLEY
Maralal
EASTERN
Habaswein
Lagh Bor
Lagh Dima
Bu'aale

Bungoma
Tombach
Eldoret
2500
Lake Baringo
Ewaso Ngiro
Isiolo
Mado Gashi
Hagadera
Jilib

WESTERN
Kakamega
Kapsabet
Nyahururu
Nanyuki
Nyambeni Hills
Meru
Equator

0° Kisumu
Nakuru
Aberdare Range
3999 ▲
Nyeri
▲ *Mt Kenya* 5199
Tana
Garissa

Winam Gulf
Kericho
Mau 3080 ▲
Gilgil
Embu
Bura

Homa Bay
Kisii
L. Naivasha
CENTRAL
Masinga Res.
Galole

NYANZA
Narok
Ewaso Ngiro
Thika
Kitui
Kathua
Kaambooni

Magadi
Nairobi ■ NAIROBI
Athi River
Athi Plains
Machakos
Yata Plateau
Galana
INDIAN OCEAN

2

Lake Natron
Namanga
Chyulu Range
Athi
Garsen
Pate I.
Lamu I.
Kipini
Ungwana Bay

Loolmalasin 3648 ▲
Meru 4565 ▲
5895 Kilimanjaro ▲
Tsavo
COAST
Malindi

TANZANIA
L. Eyasi
Lake Manyara
Moshi
Hai
L. Jipe
Arusha ✈
Voi
Kilifi

Serengeti Plains
Taita Hills
Mombasa ✈

Lushoto
Kwale

1

Tanga
Pemba Channel
Pemba I.

Zanzibar
Ras Nungwi

Zanzibar I.
Ras Kizimkazi
Zanzibar Channel

Dar es Salaam

40°E · C

FACTS ABOUT KENYA

LANDSCAPE
Area: 580 367 sq km
Highest point: 5199 m

POPULATION
Total: 30 340 000
Density: 52 persons per sq km

SETTLEMENT
% Urban population: 20
Main towns/cities: Nairobi, Mombasa

LAND USE
Main crops: Tea, coffee
Main industries: Food processing, petroleum products, chemicals, cement

DEVELOPMENT INDICATORS
Life expectancy: male 48, female 49
GNP per capita: US$ 350
Primary school enrolment ratio: 91
% Access to safe water: 53

KEY

	over 5000 m
	3000 – 5000 m
	2000 – 3000 m
	1000 – 2000 m
	500 – 1000 m
	200 – 500 m
	0 – 200 m

5199 ▲ Mountain height (height in metres)

River
Seasonal River
Lake
Seasonal lake
Country boundary
Disputed boundary
Regional boundary
Road
Railway
✈ Airport
■ Capital city
● Large town or city
○ Other town or city

Scale 1 : 5 000 000

0 50 100 150 200 km

Oblated Stereographic projection

ANNUAL RAINFALL

The heaviest rain falls in April and May. The highlands and western areas receive ample rainfall but most of the north and northeast is very dry.

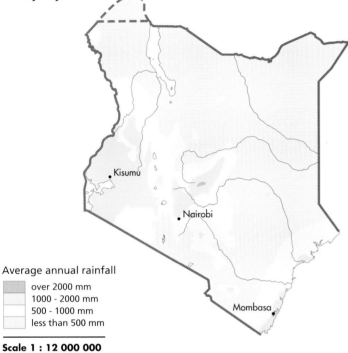

Average annual rainfall

	over 2000 mm
	1000 - 2000 mm
	500 - 1000 mm
	less than 500 mm

Scale 1 : 12 000 000

CLIMATE STATISTICS

Kenya has a tropical climate which varies with altitude. The coastal lowland area is hot and humid but the highlands region is much drier and cooler.

Nairobi	Jan	Feb	Mar	Apr	May	Jun	Jul	Aug	Sep	Oct	Nov	Dec
Temperature -°C	20	21	21	20	19	18	17	17	19	20	19	19
Rainfall - mm	49	36	85	153	126	32	13	18	21	48	132	75

Mombasa	Jan	Feb	Mar	Apr	May	Jun	Jul	Aug	Sep	Oct	Nov	Dec
Temperature -°C	28	28	28	28	26	25	24	24	25	26	27	28
Rainfall - mm	17	10	30	108	149	54	34	47	46	62	66	32

Kisumu	Jan	Feb	Mar	Apr	May	Jun	Jul	Aug	Sep	Oct	Nov	Dec
Temperature -°C	24	24	24	23	23	22	22	22	23	24	24	23
Rainfall - mm	62	88	163	207	173	93	63	90	82	72	111	107

VEGETATION

Large areas of Kenya are covered in sparsely wooded Savanna. The most varied vegetation is found in the highlands where Savanna gives way to woodland and forest. North of the river Tana semi desert areas support little vegetation.

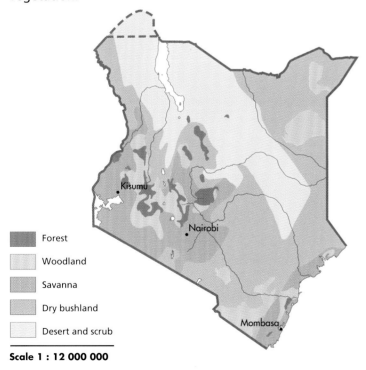

	Forest
	Woodland
	Savanna
	Dry bushland
	Desert and scrub

Scale 1 : 12 000 000

POPULATION

Kenya's population is distributed very unevenly. The most densely populated areas are found in areas with adequate rainfall. The main urban settlements are Nairobi and Mombasa. The dry north and northeast areas are sparsely populated as lack of water limits the development of any settlement.

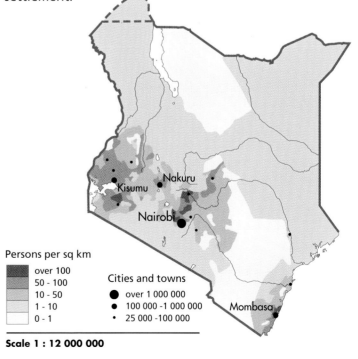

Persons per sq km

	over 100
	50 - 100
	10 - 50
	1 - 10
	0 - 1

Cities and towns
- ● over 1 000 000
- ● 100 000 -1 000 000
- • 25 000 -100 000

Scale 1 : 12 000 000

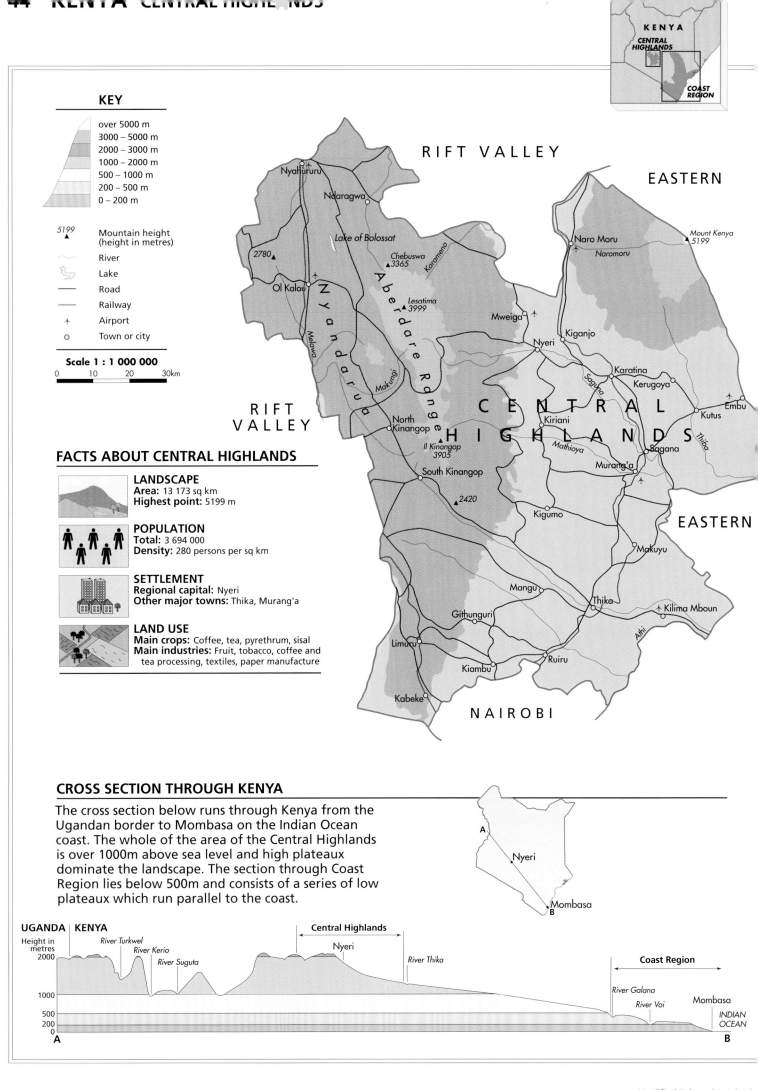

KEY

over 5000 m
3000 – 5000 m
2000 – 3000 m
1000 – 2000 m
500 – 1000 m
200 – 500 m
0 – 200 m

5199 ▲ Mountain height (height in metres)

〰 River

🦢 Lake

── Road

── Railway

✈ Airport

o Town or city

Scale 1 : 1 000 000

0   10   20   30km

FACTS ABOUT CENTRAL HIGHLANDS

LANDSCAPE
Area: 13 173 sq km
Highest point: 5199 m

POPULATION
Total: 3 694 000
Density: 280 persons per sq km

SETTLEMENT
Regional capital: Nyeri
Other major towns: Thika, Murang'a

LAND USE
Main crops: Coffee, tea, pyrethrum, sisal
Main industries: Fruit, tobacco, coffee and tea processing, textiles, paper manufacture

RIFT VALLEY

EASTERN

KENYA
CENTRAL HIGHLANDS

COAST REGION

Nyahururu
Ndaragwa
Lake of Bolossat
2780 ▲
Chebuswa 3365 ▲
Ol Kalou
Lesatima 3999 ▲
Naro Moru
Naromoru
Mount Kenya 5199 ▲
Mweiga
Kiganjo
Nyeri
Karamena
Karatina
Kerugoya
Saguha
Embu
Kutus
Kiriani
North Kinangop
Il Kinangop 3905 ▲
Mathioya
Murang'a
Sagana
Thiba
South Kinangop
2420 ▲
Kigumo
Makuyu
Mangu
Githunguri
Thika
Kilima Mboun
Limuru
Ruiru
Athi
Kiambu
Kabeke

RIFT VALLEY

CENTRAL HIGHLANDS

EASTERN

NAIROBI

CROSS SECTION THROUGH KENYA

The cross section below runs through Kenya from the Ugandan border to Mombasa on the Indian Ocean coast. The whole of the area of the Central Highlands is over 1000m above sea level and high plateaux dominate the landscape. The section through Coast Region lies below 500m and consists of a series of low plateaux which run parallel to the coast.

A
Nyeri

Mombasa
B

UGANDA | KENYA
Height in metres

Central Highlands
Nyeri

2000
River Turkwel
River Kerio
River Suguta
River Thika

Coast Region

1000
River Galana
River Voi
Mombasa

500
200
0

INDIAN OCEAN

A   B

Modified Polyconic projection

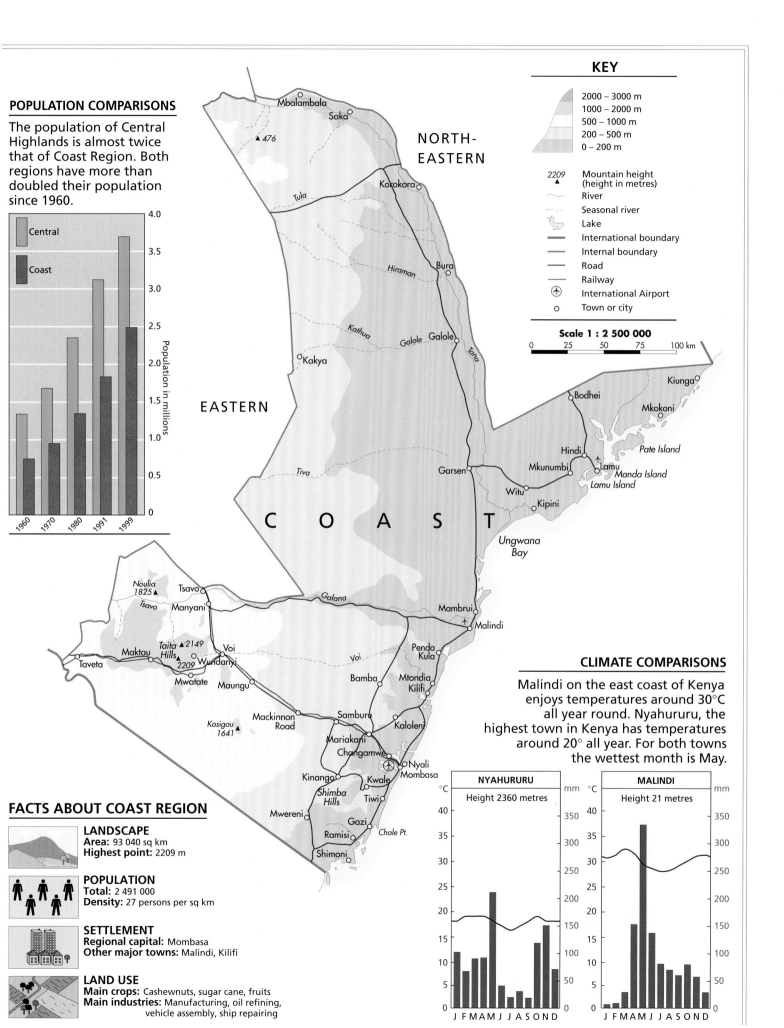

POPULATION COMPARISONS

The population of Central Highlands is almost twice that of Coast Region. Both regions have more than doubled their population since 1960.

Central
Coast

Population in millions

4.0
3.5
3.0
2.5
2.0
1.5
1.0
0.5
0

1960 1970 1980 1991 1999

KEY

2000 – 3000 m
1000 – 2000 m
500 – 1000 m
200 – 500 m
0 – 200 m

2209 ▲ Mountain height (height in metres)

〜 River

Seasonal river

Lake

International boundary

Internal boundary

Road

Railway

✈ International Airport

○ Town or city

Scale 1 : 2 500 000

0 25 50 75 100 km

NORTH-EASTERN

EASTERN

C O A S T

Mbalambala
Saka
▲ 476
Korokora
Tula
Hiraman
Bura
Kathua
Galole Galole
Tana
Kakya
Tiva
Garsen
Bodhei
Kiunga
Mkokoni
Pate Island
Hindi
Mkunumbi
Lamu
Manda Island
Witu
Lamu Island
Kipini
Ungwana Bay
Galana
Mambrui
Malindi
Noulia 1825 ▲
Tsavo
Tsavo
Manyani
Penda Kula
Taita ▲ 2149 Hills ▲ 2209
Voi
Voi
Mtondia Kilifi
Maktau
Wundanyi
Bamba
Taveta
Mwatate
Maungu
Samburu
Kaloleni
Mackinnon Road
Kasigau 1641 ▲
Mariakani
Changamwe
Kinango
Nyali Mombasa
Kwale
Shimba Hills
Tiwi
Mwereni
Gazi
Chale Pt.
Ramisi
Shimoni

CLIMATE COMPARISONS

Malindi on the east coast of Kenya enjoys temperatures around 30°C all year round. Nyahururu, the highest town in Kenya has temperatures around 20° all year. For both towns the wettest month is May.

NYAHURURU
Height 2360 metres
°C mm
40 350
35 300
30 250
25 200
20 150
15 100
10 50
5
0 0
J F M A M J J A S O N D

MALINDI
Height 21 metres
°C mm
40 350
35 300
30 250
25 200
15 150
10 100
5 50
0 0
J F M A M J J A S O N D

FACTS ABOUT COAST REGION

LANDSCAPE
Area: 93 040 sq km
Highest point: 2209 m

POPULATION
Total: 2 491 000
Density: 27 persons per sq km

SETTLEMENT
Regional capital: Mombasa
Other major towns: Malindi, Kilifi

LAND USE
Main crops: Cashewnuts, sugar cane, fruits
Main industries: Manufacturing, oil refining, vehicle assembly, ship repairing

TOURISM

Tourism makes an important contribution to Kenya's economy. The main attractions are wildlife in the National Parks and National Reserves, and the resorts on the Indian Ocean coast. The temperature is over 20°C throughout the country all year.

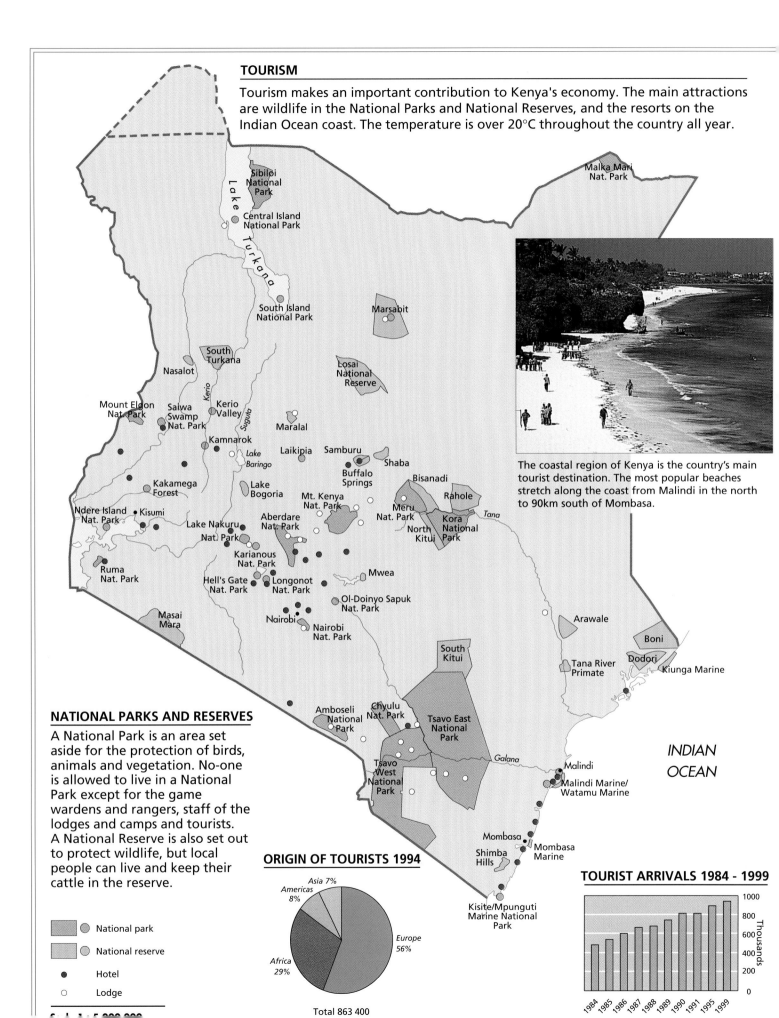

Malka Mari Nat. Park

Sibiloi National Park

Central Island National Park

Lake Turkana

South Island National Park

Marsabit

South Turkana

Nasalot

Losai National Reserve

Mount Elgon Nat. Park

Saiwa Swamp Nat. Park

Kerio Valley

Kerio

Maralal

Kamnarok

Suguta

Laikipia

Samburu

Shaba

Lake Baringo

Buffalo Springs

Bisanadi

Kakamega Forest

Lake Bogoria

Mt. Kenya Nat. Park

Meru Nat. Park

Rahole

Ndere Island Nat. Park

Kisumi

Lake Nakuru Nat. Park

Aberdare Nat. Park

North Kitui

Kora National Park

Tana

Ruma Nat. Park

Karianous Nat. Park

Hell's Gate Nat. Park

Longonot Nat. Park

Mwea

Ol-Doinyo Sapuk Nat. Park

Arawale

Masai Mara

Nairobi

Nairobi Nat. Park

Boni

Dodori

Tana River Primate

Kiunga Marine

South Kitui

Amboseli National Park

Chyulu Nat. Park

Tsavo East National Park

Galana

Malindi

INDIAN OCEAN

Tsavo West National Park

Malindi Marine/ Watamu Marine

The coastal region of Kenya is the country's main tourist destination. The most popular beaches stretch along the coast from Malindi in the north to 90km south of Mombasa.

Mombasa

Shimba Hills

Mombasa Marine

Kisite/Mpunguti Marine National Park

NATIONAL PARKS AND RESERVES

A National Park is an area set aside for the protection of birds, animals and vegetation. No-one is allowed to live in a National Park except for the game wardens and rangers, staff of the lodges and camps and tourists. A National Reserve is also set out to protect wildlife, but local people can live and keep their cattle in the reserve.

National park

National reserve

● Hotel

○ Lodge

ORIGIN OF TOURISTS 1994

Asia 7%
Americas 8%
Europe 56%
Africa 29%

Total 863 400

TOURIST ARRIVALS 1984 - 1999

Thousands

1000
800
600
400
200
0

1984 1985 1986 1987 1988 1989 1990 1991 1995 1999

MASAI MARA NATIONAL RESERVE

Situated on the border with Tanzania, the Masai Mara National Reserve is one of Kenya's best known wildlife reserves. Animals such as gazelles, elephants, cheetahs, buffalo and a few black rhino live here all year round. During July and October over one million wildebeest and a quarter of a million zebra move through the Masai Mara on their migrations from and to the Serengeti in Tanzania.

Hot air balloon flights over the plains in the Masai Mara are a popular way of viewing the herds of wildlife.

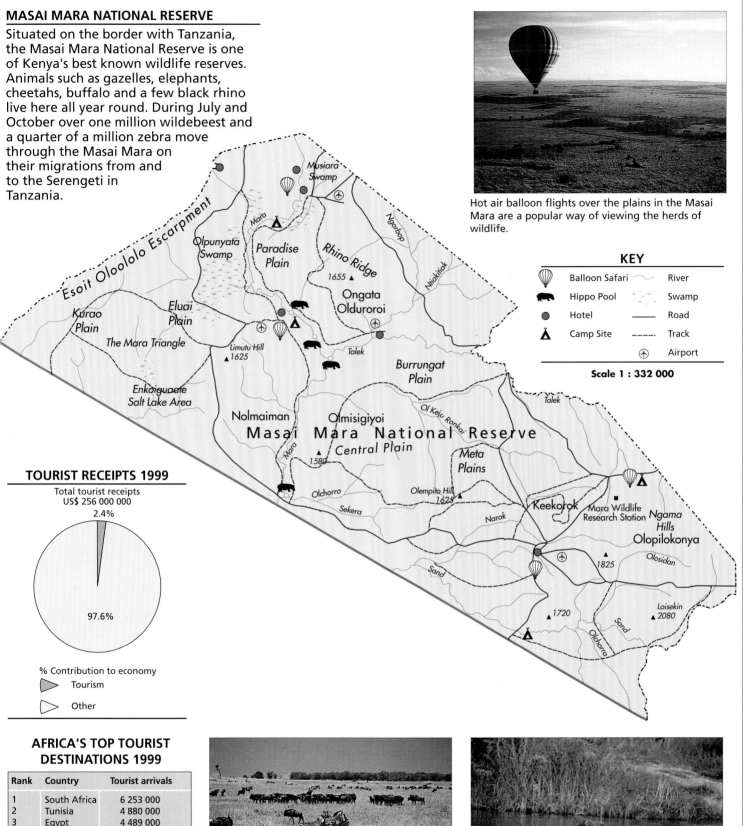

KEY

🎈	Balloon Safari	∿	River
🦛	Hippo Pool	⋰	Swamp
●	Hotel	——	Road
⛺	Camp Site	-----	Track
		✈	Airport

Scale 1 : 332 000

TOURIST RECEIPTS 1999

Total tourist receipts
US$ 256 000 000

2.4%

97.6%

% Contribution to economy
▷ Tourism
▷ Other

AFRICA'S TOP TOURIST DESTINATIONS 1999

Rank	Country	Tourist arrivals
1	South Africa	6 253 000
2	Tunisia	4 880 000
3	Egypt	4 489 000
4	Morocco	3 824 000
5	Zimbabwe	2 328 000
6	**Kenya**	**943 000**
7	Algeria	755 000
8	Botswana	740 000
9	Nigeria	739 000
10	Mauritius	578 000
11	Namibia	560 000
12	Zambia	456 000
13	Tanzania	450 000
14	Reunion	402 000
15	Ghana	335 000

For four months every year herds of wildebeest from Tanzania graze on the Mara plains. Tall grasses are reduced to stubble before the herds trek south again.

Hippos can be found wallowing in pools in the Mara river.

KEY

- over 5000 m
- 3000 – 5000 m
- 2000 – 3000 m
- 1000 – 2000 m
- 500 – 1000 m
- 200 – 500 m
- 0 – 200 m
- land below sea level

Ice Cap

6194 ▲ Mountain height
(height in metres)

Scale 1 : 40 000 000

0   400   800   1200   1600 km

Chamberlin Trimetric projection

This is a false colour image of North and Central America and Greenland. The different colours have been chosen to highlight the many different environments of the region. The cold areas, often with permanent snow and ice, are shown in pale grey, whilst the frozen sea ice of the Arctic Ocean is grey-green. The tundra areas are shown in yellow. The prairies are highlighted in brownish reds whilst the dark reds show areas of rich grasslands and deciduous forest.

The Arctic tundra is a cold region with no trees and soils that are often frozen.

Frozen sea ice in the Arctic Ocean.

Greenland is mostly covered by snow and ice.

The dark reds show grassland and forest areas.

The Prairie grasslands stretch from Canada to the southern USA.

There are high mountains along the whole west coast of North America.

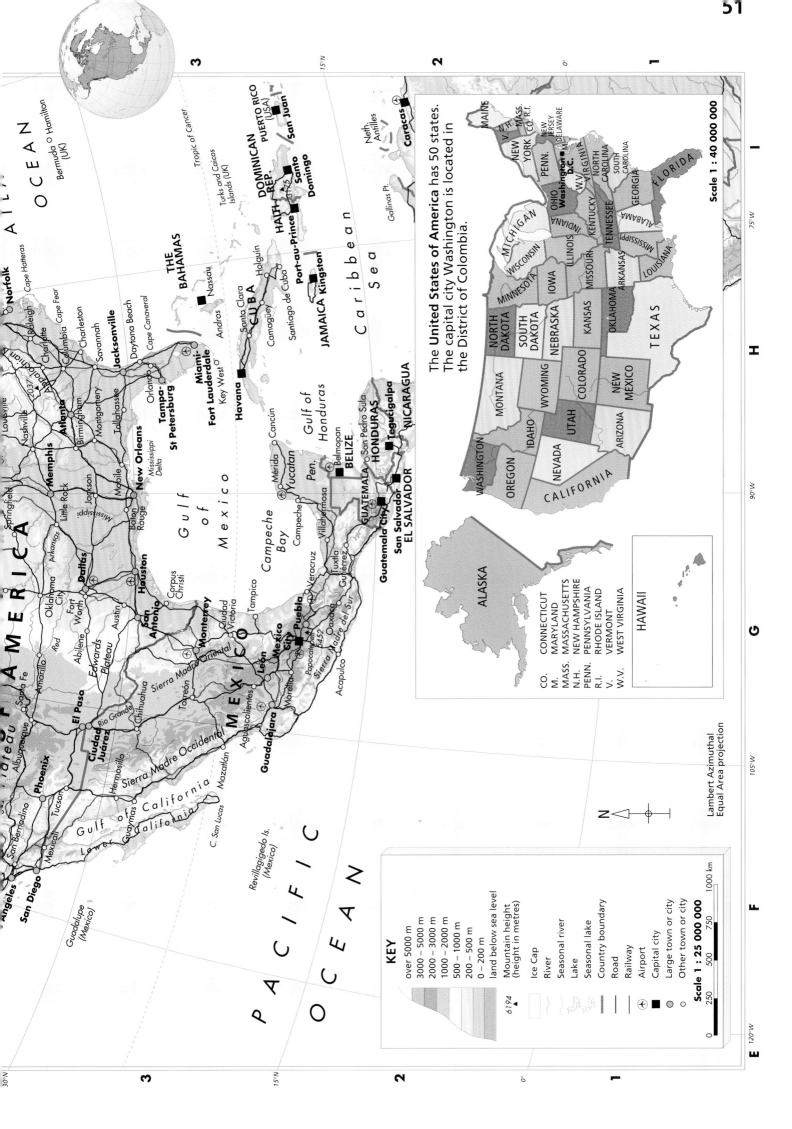

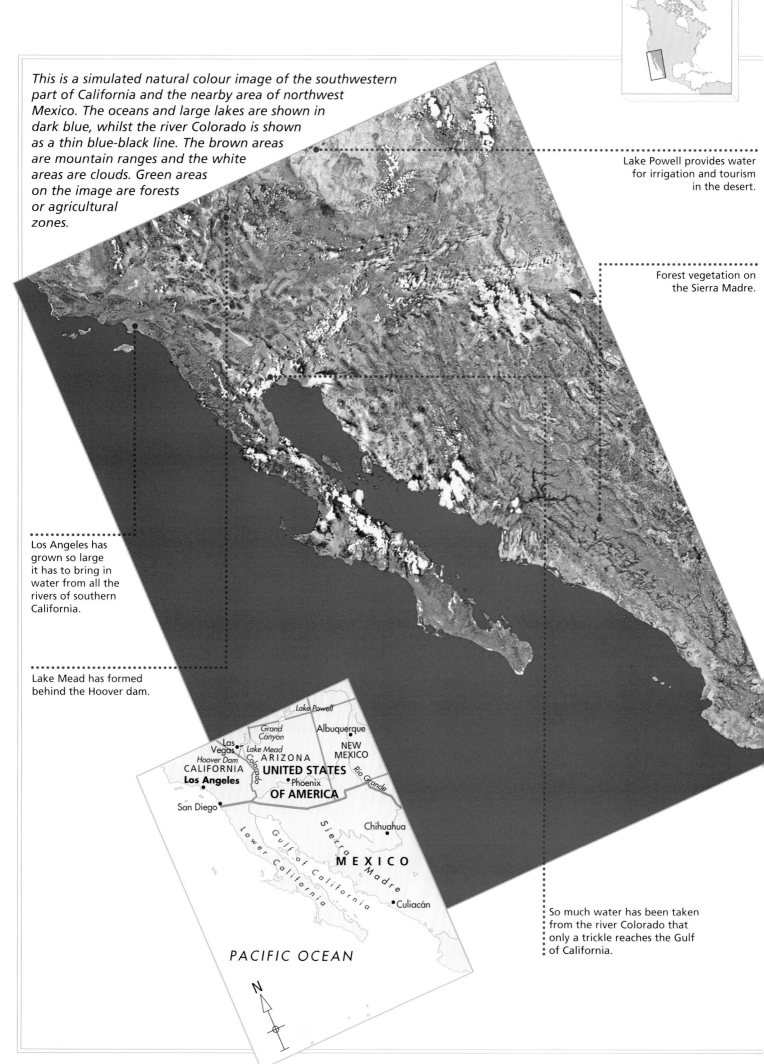

This is a simulated natural colour image of the southwestern part of California and the nearby area of northwest Mexico. The oceans and large lakes are shown in dark blue, whilst the river Colorado is shown as a thin blue-black line. The brown areas are mountain ranges and the white areas are clouds. Green areas on the image are forests or agricultural zones.

Lake Powell provides water for irrigation and tourism in the desert.

Forest vegetation on the Sierra Madre.

Los Angeles has grown so large it has to bring in water from all the rivers of southern California.

Lake Mead has formed behind the Hoover dam.

So much water has been taken from the river Colorado that only a trickle reaches the Gulf of California.

Lake Powell
Grand Canyon
Albuquerque
Las Vegas
Lake Mead
NEW MEXICO
Hoover Dam
ARIZONA
CALIFORNIA
UNITED STATES
Los Angeles
OF AMERICA
Colorado
Phoenix
Rio Grande
San Diego
Chihuahua
MEXICO
Lower California
Gulf of California
Sierra Madre
Culiacán
PACIFIC OCEAN

N

Florida

This is a simulated natural colour image showing Hurricane Fran approaching Florida and the Caribbean on 4th September 1996. The hurricane stands out as the white swirl of cloud. The yellow-white centre shows the part of the storm where the wind is strongest. The hurricane had winds of up to 190 kph and killed 34 people. The green areas are land and the black areas are sea. The middle clouds of the hurricane are a blue-grey colour. Hurricane Fran hit land at Cape Fear in North Carolina on 5th September 1996.

N

Cuba

The eye or centre of the hurricane.

HURRICANE TRACKS

Hurricanes originate in the warm, moist tropical air over the Atlantic Ocean and move westwards at about 20 kph. Their power declines rapidly as they pass over land or cooler water and they usually last for about 9 days.

HURRICANE RISK

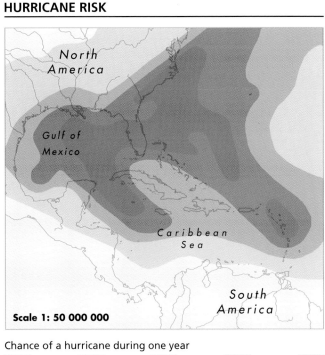

Scale 1: 50 000 000

Chance of a hurricane during one year

| less than 5% | 5-35% | 35-55% | 55-65% | 65-90% |

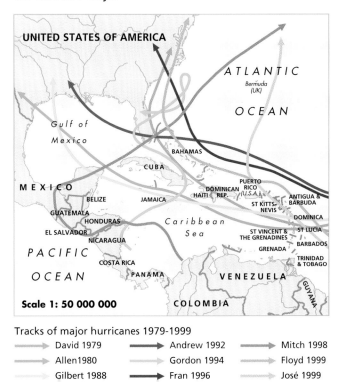

Scale 1: 50 000 000

Tracks of major hurricanes 1979-1999

David 1979   Andrew 1992   Mitch 1998
Allen 1980   Gordon 1994   Floyd 1999
Gilbert 1988   Fran 1996   José 1999

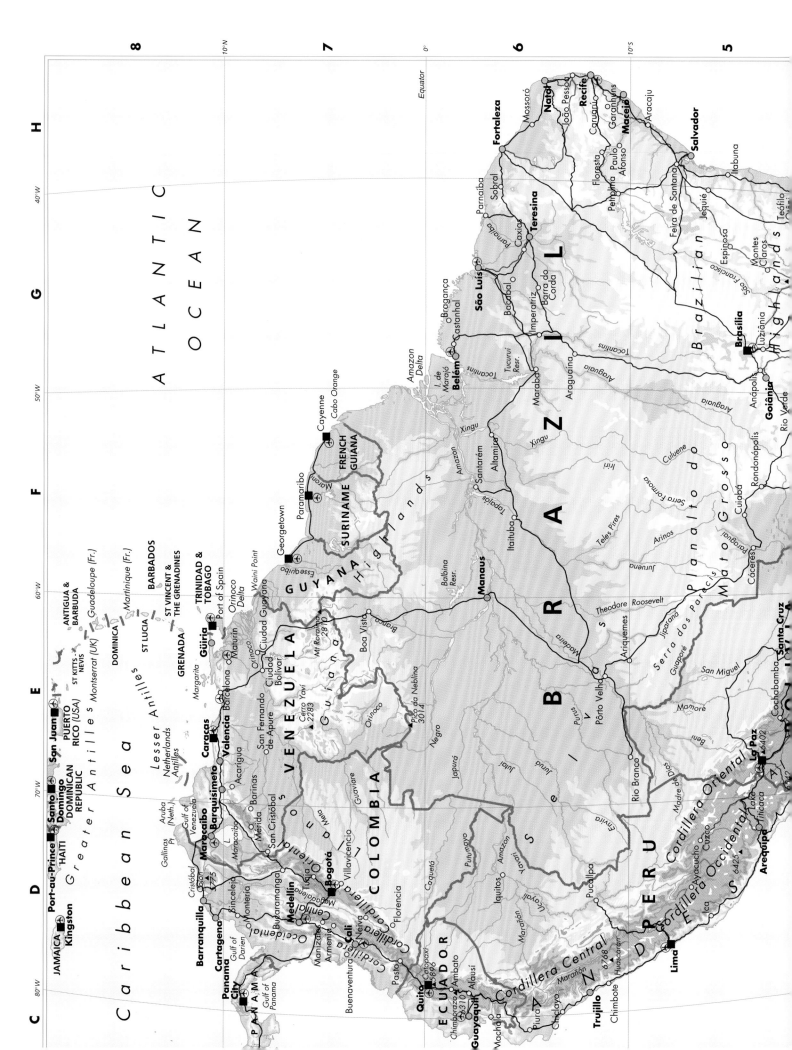

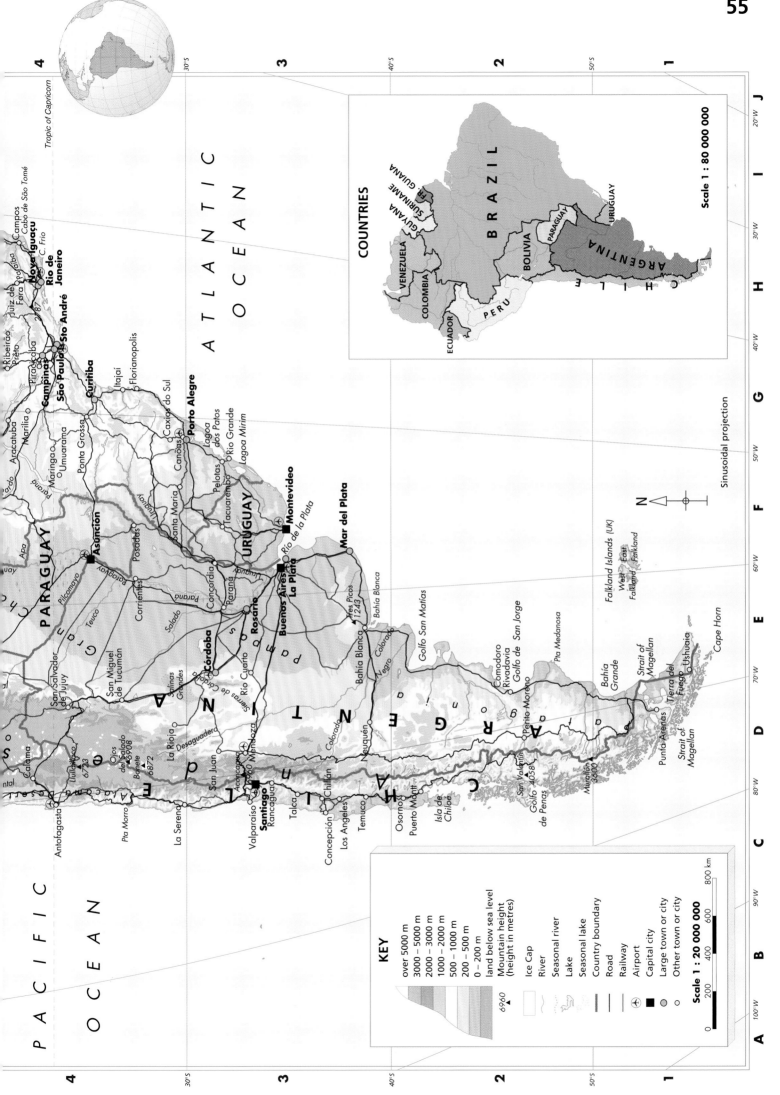

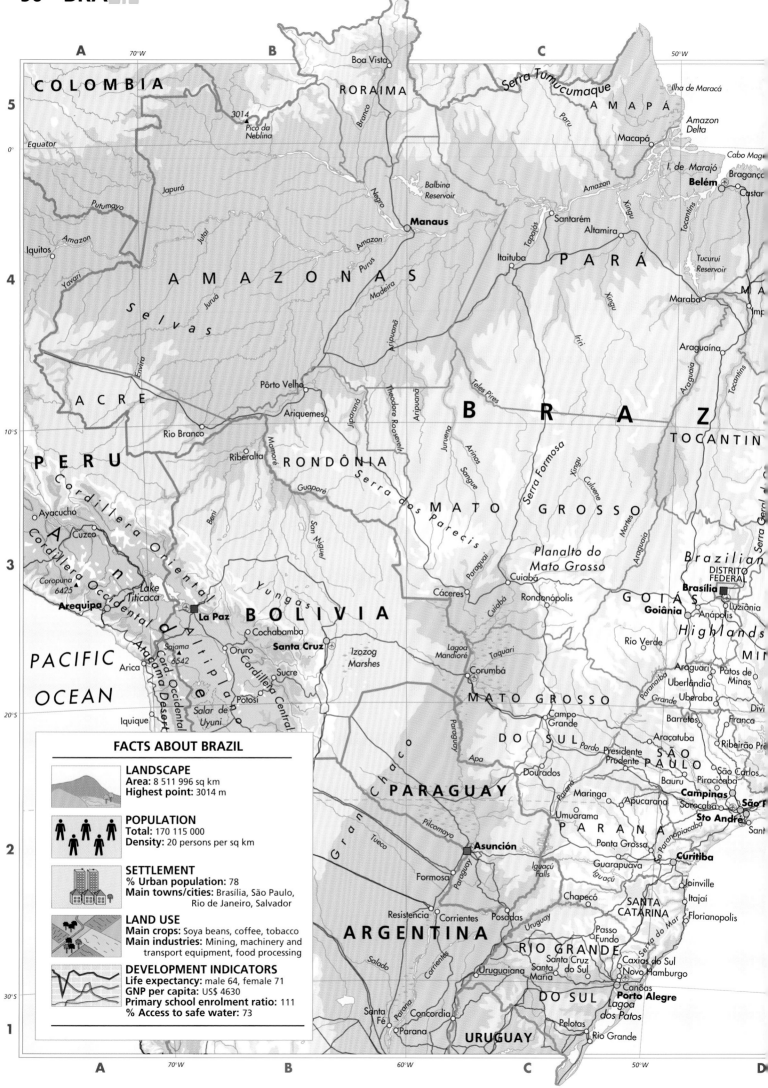

COLOMBIA

RORAIMA

Boa Vista

Serra Tumucumaque

AMAPÁ

Ilha de Maracá

Amazon Delta

Macapá

Cabo Mag

Equator

Pico da Neblina 3014

Branco

I. de Marajó

Belém

Bragança

Castar

Iquitos

Japurá

Putumayo

Amazon

Yavari

A M A Z O N A S

Manaus

Amazon

Santarém

Altamira

Xingu

P A R Á

Tucuruí Reservoir

MA

Juruá

S e l v a s

Purus

Madeira

Itaituba

Tapajós

Imp

A C R E

Jutaí

Envira

Pôrto Velho

Aripuanã

Maraba

Araguaína

Theodore Roosevelt

Irri

Xingu

B R A Z

P E R U

Ariquemes

Jiparaná

Teles Pires

Juruena

Serra Formosa

Xingu

Culuene

TOCANTIN

10°S

Rio Branco

Riberalta

R O N D Ô N I A

Mamoré

Guaporé

Serra dos Parecis

M A T O   G R O S S O

Arinos

Sangue

Mortes

Araguaia

Tocantins

Ayacucho

Cuzco

Beni

San Miguel

Y u n g a s

Paraguai

Planalto do Mato Grosso

Serra Gerral do

Coropuna 6425

Lake Titicaca

B O L I V I A

Cáceres

Cuiabá

Cuiabá

Rondonópolis

B r a z i l i a n

DISTRITO FEDERAL

Brasília

G O I Á S

Arequipa

La Paz

Cochabamba

Santa Cruz

Goiânia

Luziânia

Anápolis

H i g h l a n d s

Sajama 6542

Oruro

Sucre

Izozog Marshes

Lagoa Mandioré

Taquari

Rio Verde

MIN

Corumbá

Araguari

Patos de Minas

Arica

Cordillera Central

Potosí

Uberlândia

Uberaba

PACIFIC OCEAN

Salar de Uyuni

Paraguay

M A T O   G R O S S O

Paranaíba

Grande

Divi

Iquique

Campo Grande

D O   S U L

Pardo

Barretos

Franca

Araçatuba

Ribeirão Pr

20°S

Apa

Presidente Prudente

S Ã O

São Carlos

Dourados

Paraná

Bauru

Piracicaba

P A U L O

FACTS ABOUT BRAZIL

LANDSCAPE
Area: 8 511 996 sq km
Highest point: 3014 m

Maringa

Apucarana

Campinas

São P

Sorocaba

Sto André

C h a c o

P A R A G U A Y

Umuarama

P A R A N Á

POPULATION
Total: 170 115 000
Density: 20 persons per sq km

Pilcomayo

Asunción

Ponta Grossa

Curitiba

Tueco

Formosa

Guarapuava

Iguaçu Falls

Joinville

SETTLEMENT
% Urban population: 78
Main towns/cities: Brasília, São Paulo, Rio de Janeiro, Salvador

Iguaçu

Itajaí

Chapecó

SANTA CATARINA

Florianopolis

LAND USE
Main crops: Soya beans, coffee, tobacco
Main industries: Mining, machinery and transport equipment, food processing

Resistencia

Corrientes

Posadas

Uruguay

Passo Fundo

RIO GRANDE

Caxias do Sul

Novo Hamburgo

Canôas

DEVELOPMENT INDICATORS
Life expectancy: male 64, female 71
GNP per capita: US$ 4630
Primary school enrolment ratio: 111
% Access to safe water: 73

A R G E N T I N A

Salado

Corrientes

Uruguaiana

Santa Cruz do Sul

Santa Maria

D O   S U L

Porto Alegre

Lagoa dos Patos

30°S

Santa Fé

Parana

Concordia

Pelotas

Rio Grande

URUGUAY

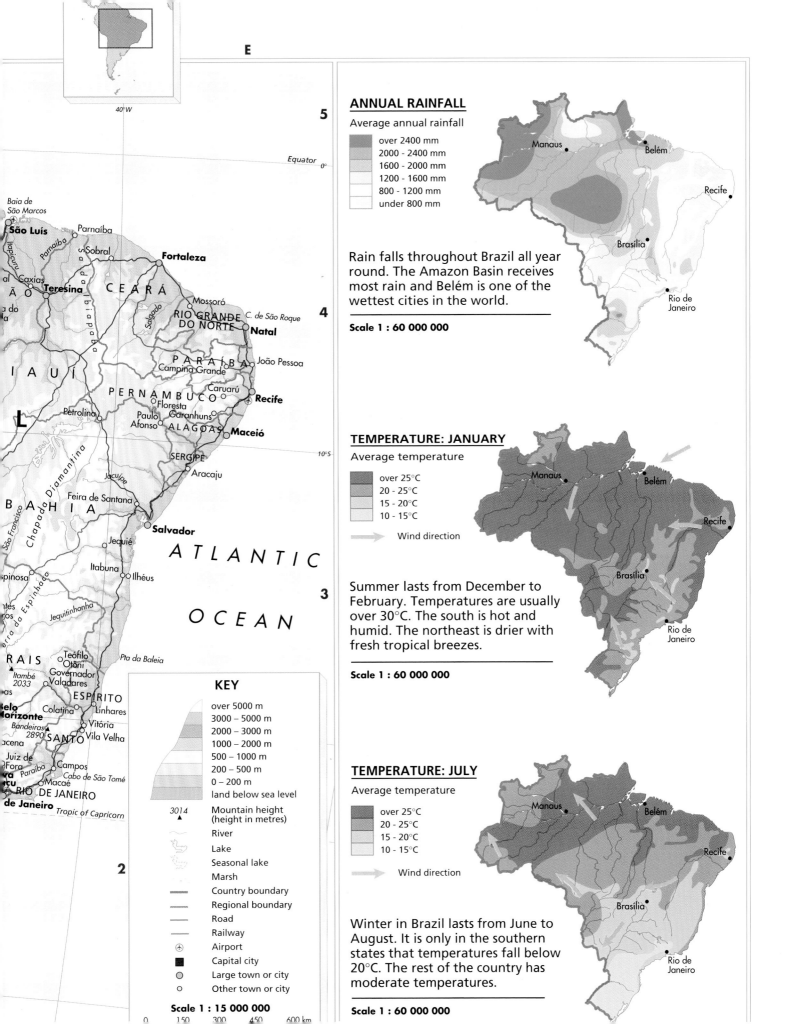

E

40°W

Equator 0°

5

ANNUAL RAINFALL

Average annual rainfall

- over 2400 mm
- 2000 – 2400 mm
- 1600 – 2000 mm
- 1200 – 1600 mm
- 800 – 1200 mm
- under 800 mm

Manaus
Belém
Recife
Brasília
Rio de Janeiro

Rain falls throughout Brazil all year round. The Amazon Basin receives most rain and Belém is one of the wettest cities in the world.

Scale 1 : 60 000 000

4

Baia de São Marcos
São Luís
Parnaíba
Itapicuru
Parnaíba
Sobral
Fortaleza
Caxias
Teresina
CEARÁ
Mossoró
C. de São Roque
RIO GRANDE DO NORTE
Natal
PARAÍBA
João Pessoa
Campina Grande
PERNAMBUCO
Caruarú
Recife
Petrolina
Floresta
Garanhuns
Paulo Afonso
ALAGOAS
Maceió
SERGIPE
Aracaju
Jacuípe
Feira de Santana
BAHIA
São Francisco
Chapada Diamantina
Salvador
Jequié
Itabuna
Ilhéus
Jequitinhonha
Serra da Espinhaço
Pta da Baleia

10°S

ATLANTIC OCEAN

3

PIAUÍ
L
ÃO

TEMPERATURE: JANUARY

Average temperature

- over 25°C
- 20 – 25°C
- 15 – 20°C
- 10 – 15°C
- Wind direction

Manaus
Belém
Recife
Brasília
Rio de Janeiro

Summer lasts from December to February. Temperatures are usually over 30°C. The south is hot and humid. The northeast is drier with fresh tropical breezes.

Scale 1 : 60 000 000

Teófilo Otóni
Itambé 2033
Governador Valadares
ESPIRITO
Colatina
Linhares
Belo Horizonte
Bandeiras 2890
Vitória
Vila Velha
SANTO
Juiz de Fora
Paraíba
Campos
Cabo de São Tomé
Macaé
RIO DE JANEIRO
de Janeiro
Tropic of Capricorn
RAIS

KEY

- over 5000 m
- 3000 – 5000 m
- 2000 – 3000 m
- 1000 – 2000 m
- 500 – 1000 m
- 200 – 500 m
- 0 – 200 m
- land below sea level

▲ 3014   Mountain height (height in metres)

River

Lake

Seasonal lake

Marsh

Country boundary

Regional boundary

Road

Railway

⊕ Airport

■ Capital city

● Large town or city

○ Other town or city

Scale 1 : 15 000 000

0   150   300   450   600 km

2

TEMPERATURE: JULY

Average temperature

- over 25°C
- 20 – 25°C
- 15 – 20°C
- 10 – 15°C
- Wind direction

Manaus
Belém
Recife
Brasília
Rio de Janeiro

Winter in Brazil lasts from June to August. It is only in the southern states that temperatures fall below 20°C. The rest of the country has moderate temperatures.

Scale 1 : 60 000 000

KEY

	1000 – 2000 m
	500 – 1000 m
	200 – 500 m
	0 – 200 m
1123 ▲	Mountain height (height in metres)
	River
	Seasonal river
	Lake
	Internal boundary
	Road
	Railway
✈	Airport
◉	Large town or city
○	Other town or city

Scale 1 : 4 500 000

0   50   100   150km

N

Map labels

Camocim, Granja, Acaraú, Acaraú, Itapipoca, Paracuru, Sobral, Tianguá, Fortaleza, Caucaia, Aquiraz, Maranguape, Cascavel, Santa Quitéria, Canindé, Baturité, Ipu, Serra Baturité, Aracati, Quixadá, Morada Nova, Areia Branca, Boa Viagem, Açude Banabuiu, Mossoró, Macau, Crateús, Quixeramobim, Ponta do Calcanhar, Touros, Senador Pompeu, Mombaça, Jaguaribe, Açu, Lajes, Taua, Acopiara, Açude Orós, RIO GRANDE DO NORTE, Natal, Saboeiro, Bastioes, Iguatu, Icó, Currais Novos, Sta Cruz, Canguaretama, Cuité, Campos Sales, Sousa, Piranhas, Parelhas, Curimataú, Juàzeiro do Norte, Crato, Cajázeiras, Pombal, Patos, Guarabira, Chapada do Araripe, Milagres, PARAÍBA, João Pessoa, Araripina, Gravata, Conceição, Campina Grande, Sta Rita, Ouricurí, Sumé, Timbaúba, Parnamirim, Salgueiro, Flores, Paraiba, Carpina, S. Pedro, Pajeú, Serra Talhada, Sertânia, Capiberibe, Afrânio, Cabrobó, Ouricuri, 1123, Caruarú, Jaboatão, Olinda, Recife, Floresta, Navio, Pesqueira, Arcoverde, Belo Jardim, Garças, Curaçá, Pontal, Barragem de Itaparica, Inajá, Palmares, Petrolina, Moxotó, Garanhuns, Ipojuca, Ipanema, Paulo Afonso, PERNAMBUCO, BAHIA, ALAGOAS, PIAUÍ, CEARÁ, Serra da Ibiapaba, Serra da Borborema, Planalto da Borborema, Rio da Brígida, Açude, Jaguaribe, Apodi, Salgado

ATLANTIC OCEAN

POPULATION

Since the 1960's the growth of population has been constant. Most of the population live on or near the coast.

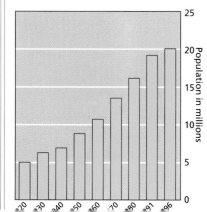

Population in millions

25
20
15
10
5
0

20 30 40 50 60 70 80 91 96

EMPLOYMENT

Northeast Brazil provides few employment opportunities in the manufacturing sector. Just over a third of the workforce make a living from agriculture.

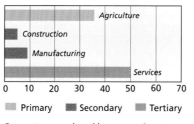

Agriculture
Construction
Manufacturing
Services

0 10 20 30 40 50 60 70

■ Primary   ■ Secondary   ■ Tertiary

FACTS ABOUT NORTHEAST COAST

LANDSCAPE
Area: 351 842 sq km
Highest point: 1123 m

POPULATION
Total: 20 072 637
Density: 57 persons per sq km

SETTLEMENT
% Urban population: 67.7
Main towns/cities: Recife, Fortaleza, Natal

LAND USE
Main crops: Haricot beans, maize, sugar cane, cashewnuts
Main industries: Engineering, chemicals, textiles, food processing

NORTHEAST COAST
B R A Z I L
SÃO PAULO

N

KEY

	2000 - 3000 m
	1000 – 2000 m
	500 – 1000 m
	200 – 500 m
	0 – 200 m

2600 ▲ Mountain height (height in metres)
~~~ River
Lake
— Internal boundary
— Road
----- Road (under construction)
— Railway
✈ Airport
◉ Large town or city
○ Other town or city

Scale 1 : 4 500 000

0   50   100   150km

MINAS GERAIS

MATO GROSSO DO SUL

Jales
Turvo
Fernandópolis
São José dos Dourados
Votuporanga
Pereira Barreto
Represa Três Irmãos
Igarapava
Franca
Barretos
Pardo
São José do Rio Prêto
Bebedouro
Ribeirão Prêto
Jaboticabal
Mococa
Pardo
Mirandópolis
Tietê
Araçatuba
Birigui
Represa Promissão
Taquaritinga
Mogi-Guaçu
Panorama
Aguapeí
Lins
Araraquara
S.João da Boa Vista
Dracena
Lucélia
S Ã O   P A U L O
São Carlos
Piraçununga
Represa Pôrto Primavera
Peixe
Presidente Prudente
Garça
Jaú
Rio Claro
Mogi-Mirim
Marília
Bauru
Limeira
2600 ▲
RIO DE JANEIRO
Teodoro Sampaio
Paranapanema
Iepê
Assis
Turvo
Piracaba
Piracicaba
Amparo
Bragança Paulista
Serra da Mantiqueira
Guaratinguetá
Campinas
Taubaté
Avaré
Jundiaí
Itu
Jacareí
S. José dos Campos
P A R A N Á
Itaí
Represa de Jurumirim
Tatuí
Sorocaba
São Paulo
Moji das Cruzes
Serra do Mar
Itapetininga
Sto André
São Bernardo do Campo
Itapeva
Capão Bonito
Juquiá
S.Vicente
Santos
Guarujá
Serra Paranapiacaba
Juquiá
Itanhaém
▲1350
Ribeira
Jacupiranga
Iguape

ATLANTIC OCEAN

POPULATION

22% of Brazil's population live in São Paulo region. Population growth has been rapid since the 1960's and the city of São Paulo is one of the world's largest cities.

Population in millions

40
35
30
25
20
15
10
5
0

1920 1930 1940 1950 1960 1970 1980 1991 1996

EMPLOYMENT

More than 60% of the region's population are employed in the service industry. However, the region contains some of Brazil's most fertile land and many of its industries are agriculture related.

Agriculture
Construction
Manufacturing
Services

0 10 20 30 40 50 60 70

■ Primary   ■ Secondary   ■ Tertiary

Percentage employed by economic sector

FACTS ABOUT SÃO PAULO REGION

LANDSCAPE
Area: 248 809 sq km
Highest point: 2600 m

POPULATION
Total: 34 119 110
Density: 137 persons per sq km

SETTLEMENT
% Urban population: 92.8
Main towns/cities: São Paulo, Campinas, Sto Andre, São Bernardo do Campo

LAND USE
Main crops: Cotton, sugar, fruit, coffee
Main industries: Motor vehicles, chemicals, textiles

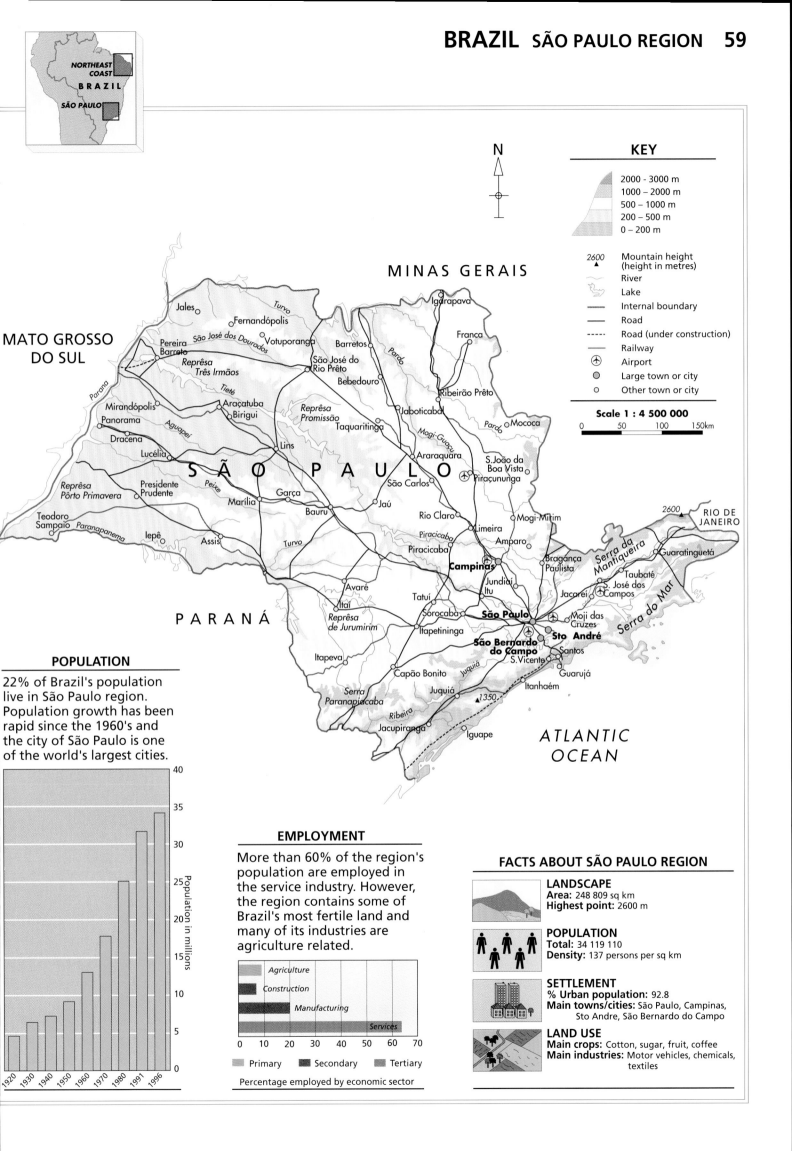

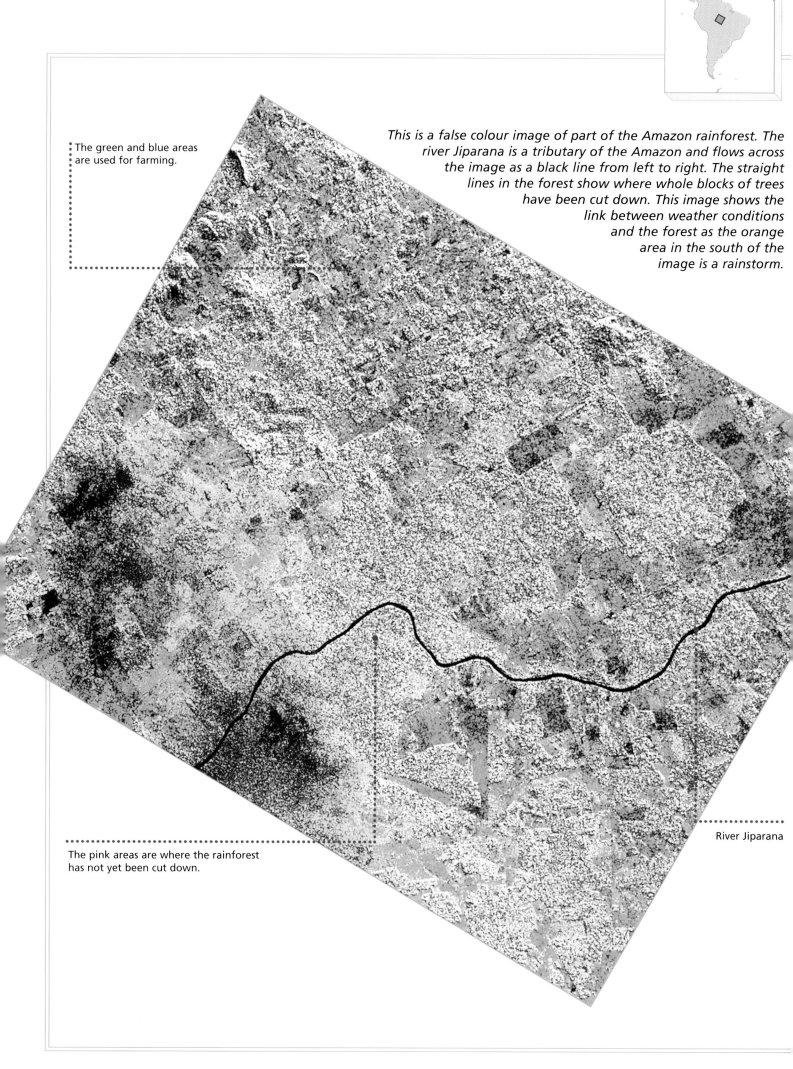

The green and blue areas are used for farming.

This is a false colour image of part of the Amazon rainforest. The river Jiparana is a tributary of the Amazon and flows across the image as a black line from left to right. The straight lines in the forest show where whole blocks of trees have been cut down. This image shows the link between weather conditions and the forest as the orange area in the south of the image is a rainstorm.

River Jiparana

The pink areas are where the rainforest has not yet been cut down.

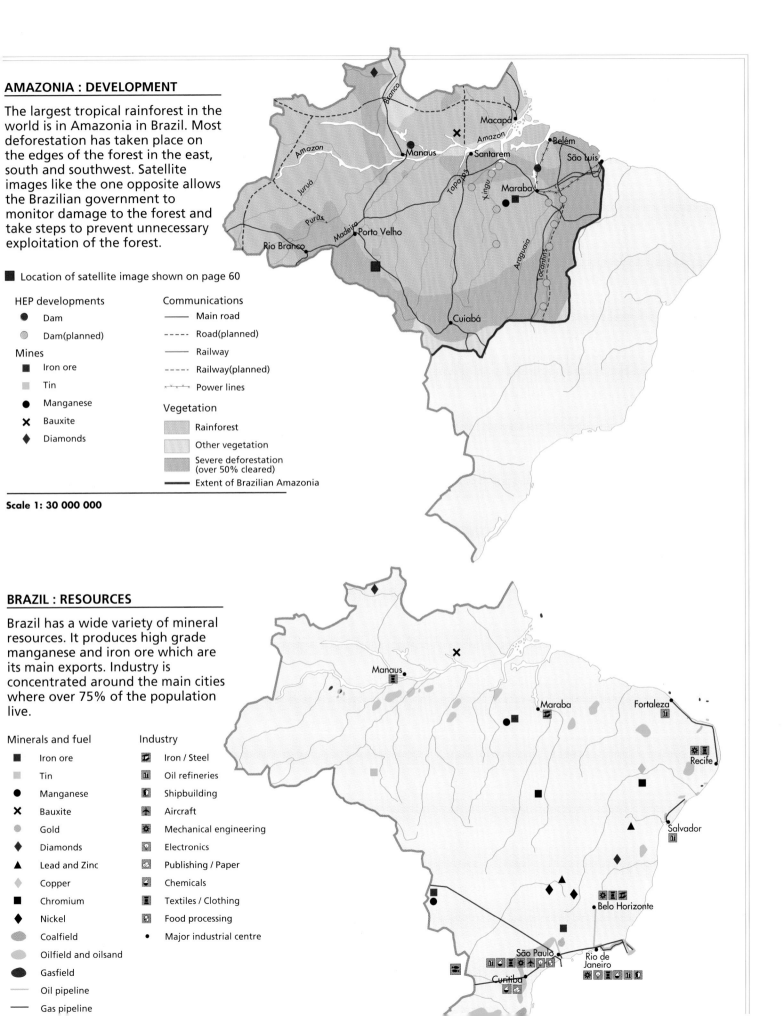

AMAZONIA : DEVELOPMENT

The largest tropical rainforest in the world is in Amazonia in Brazil. Most deforestation has taken place on the edges of the forest in the east, south and southwest. Satellite images like the one opposite allows the Brazilian government to monitor damage to the forest and take steps to prevent unnecessary exploitation of the forest.

■ Location of satellite image shown on page 60

HEP developments
- ● Dam
- ● Dam(planned)

Mines
- ■ Iron ore
- ■ Tin
- ● Manganese
- ✕ Bauxite
- ◆ Diamonds

Communications
- —— Main road
- ----- Road(planned)
- —— Railway
- ----- Railway(planned)
- ⋯⊦⋯ Power lines

Vegetation
- Rainforest
- Other vegetation
- Severe deforestation (over 50% cleared)
- —— Extent of Brazilian Amazonia

Scale 1 : 30 000 000

BRAZIL : RESOURCES

Brazil has a wide variety of mineral resources. It produces high grade manganese and iron ore which are its main exports. Industry is concentrated around the main cities where over 75% of the population live.

Minerals and fuel
- ■ Iron ore
- ■ Tin
- ● Manganese
- ✕ Bauxite
- ● Gold
- ◆ Diamonds
- ▲ Lead and Zinc
- ◆ Copper
- ■ Chromium
- ◆ Nickel
- Coalfield
- Oilfield and oilsand
- Gasfield
- Oil pipeline
- Gas pipeline

Industry
- 🏭 Iron / Steel
- 🛢 Oil refineries
- 🚢 Shipbuilding
- ✈ Aircraft
- ✳ Mechanical engineering
- 🖥 Electronics
- 📰 Publishing / Paper
- 🧪 Chemicals
- 🧵 Textiles / Clothing
- 🍲 Food processing
- • Major industrial centre

KEY

over 5000 m
3000 – 5000 m
2000 – 3000 m
1000 – 2000 m
500 – 1000 m
200 – 500 m
0 – 200 m
land below sea level

5030
▲ Mountain height
(height in metres)

Scale 1 : 30 000 000

0   400   800   1200 km

C 120°E   D 130°E   E 140°E   F 150°E   G 160°E   J

7

10°N

6

0°

10°S

5

4

20°S

3

30°S

2

Northern
Marianas
Guam Islands

Yap

C a r o l i n e   I s l a n d s

Pohnpei

Kosrae

Marshall

Bikini

Islands

Ralik Chain

Ratak Chain

P A C I F I C   O C

Nauru

Nonouti

Onoto

Gilbert
Islands

Celebes
Sea

Halmahera

Admiralty Is

Bismarck
Sea

New Ireland

New
Britain

Bougainville I.

Solomon

Islands

Sulawesi

Sula Is.

B a n d a
S e a

Maoke Range
Puncak Jaya ▲
5030

New

Guinea

Mt Wilhelm
4509 ▲

Solomon Sea

Guadalcanal

Santa Cruz
Is

Java Sea

A r a f u r a
S e a

Mt Victoria
4073 ▲

Banks Is

Timor

Torres   Strait

Espíritu Santo

V

Fiji Isla
Vir

T i m o r   S e a

Arnhem
Land

Gulf
of
Carpentaria

Cape
York
Peninsula

Great Barrier Reef

C o r a l

S e a

New
Caledonia

Loyalty
Is.

Lake Argyle

Kimberley
Plateau

Mitchell

Flinders

Great Dividing Range

P A C I F I C   O

Eighty Mile
Beach

Great Sandy
Desert

Lord Howe I

Hamersley
Range

Gibson

Desert

Macdonnell
Ranges

867
▲
Uluru
(Ayers Rock)

Simpson
Desert

A u s t r a l i a

Lake
Eyre

Darling

Ashburton

Great Victoria Desert

Lake
Torrens

Murray

Mt Kosciusko
▲ 2230

T a s m a n

North
Island

Ne

Nullarbor Plain

G r e a t

A u s t r a l i a n

B i g h t

Kangaroo I.

Bass
Strait

S e a

Zealand

Mt Cook
3754 ▲

Southern Alps

South
Island

Tasmania

S O U T H E R N

O C E A N

Auckland Is

K

7

10°N

6

N

Equator *0°*

This is a simulated natural colour image of Australia, New Zealand and the nearby parts of southeast Asia and the southwest Pacific Ocean. The desert of central and western Australia is shown in pink-brown, whilst the greens on the image show those areas with forests and farmland. Areas of grassland are shown in grey-green.

10°S

Savaii

20°S

Tongatapu Group

3

A N

ermadec Is *30°S*

2

40°S

Chatham Is

1

50°S

The centre of Australia is a hot desert. You can see some mountain ranges in the western areas.

The island of Tasmania is covered by grassland, forest and farmland.

Southeast Australia is one of the main farming areas of the country as the green colours show.

Because New Zealand is further south than Australia it is cooler and wetter. As a result there are more forests.

K *170°W*

Lambert Azimuthal Equal Area projection

KEY

over 5000 m
3000 – 5000 m
2000 – 3000 m
1000 – 2000 m
500 – 1000 m
200 – 500 m
0 – 200 m
land below sea level

3754 ▲ Mountain height (height in metres)

River

Seasonal river

Lake

Seasonal lake

━━━ Country boundary

┅┅┅ Disputed boundary

─── Regional boundary

─── Road

─── Railway

⊕ Airport

■ Capital city

◯ Large town or city

○ Other town or city

Scale 1 : 20 000 000

0   200   400   600   800 km

KIRIBATI

Gilbert
Islands

Choiseul

The Slot

Santa Isabel

SOLOMON

Malaita

TUVALU

Nui Vaitupu

Guadalcanal Honiara

ISLANDS

Nukufetau

San Cristobal

Rennell

Santa Cruz Is
(Solomon Is)

Banks Is

VANUATU

Espíritu Santo

Vanua Levu

Malakula

Éfaté

Port-Vila

Erromango

FIJI

Viti Levu

Suva

Kadavu

New
Caledonia
(Fr.) Nouméa

Loyalty
Is

P A C I F I C   O C E A N

Tropic of Capricorn

Norfolk I.
(Aust.)

Lord Howe I.
(Aust.)

A N   S E A

C. Maria van Diemen North Cape

North Island

Auckland

Manukau

Bay of
Plenty

Hamilton

East Cape

Mt Egmont
2518

N E W

Cape Farewell Palmerston
North

Napier

Z E A L A N D

Nelson

Wellington

South Island

Mt Cook
3754

Cook Str.

Southern Alps

C. Providence

L. Te Anau

Christchurch

Chatham
Is

Stewart I.

Dunedin

BUSHFIRES

In Australia bushfires are a serious hazard in the dry season especially in the southeast and southwest of the continent.

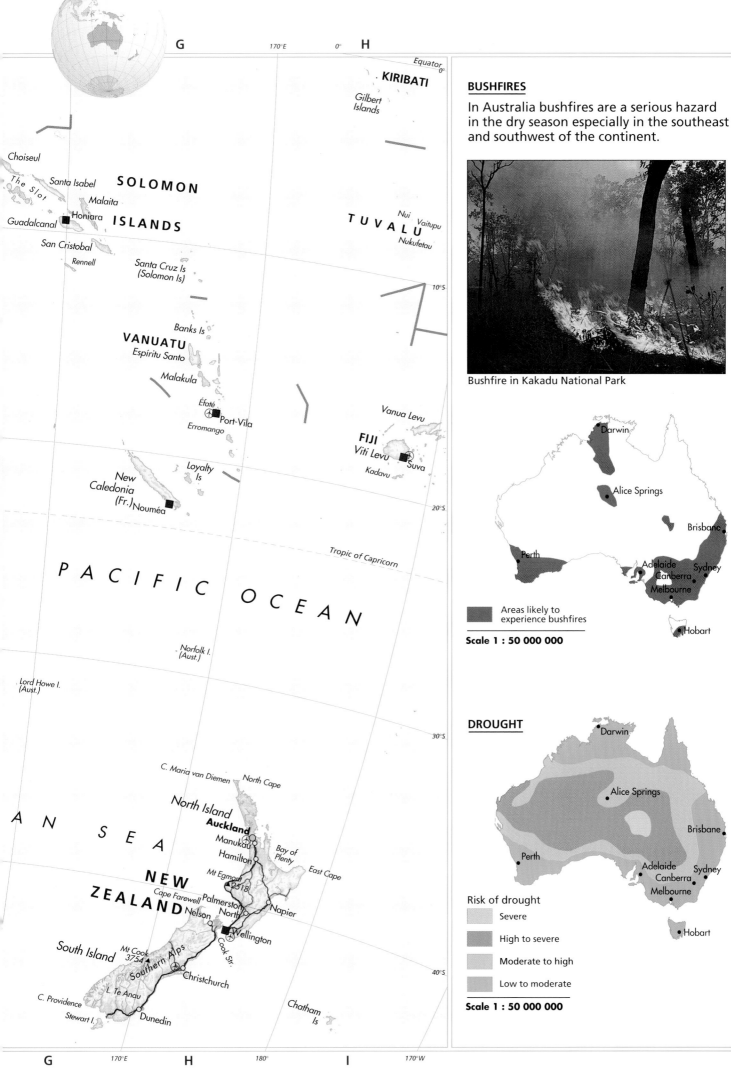

Bushfire in Kakadu National Park

Darwin

Alice Springs

Brisbane

Perth

Adelaide
Canberra Sydney
Melbourne

Hobart

Areas likely to
experience bushfires

Scale 1 : 50 000 000

DROUGHT

Darwin

Alice Springs

Brisbane

Perth

Adelaide
Canberra Sydney
Melbourne

Hobart

Risk of drought

Severe

High to severe

Moderate to high

Low to moderate

Scale 1 : 50 000 000

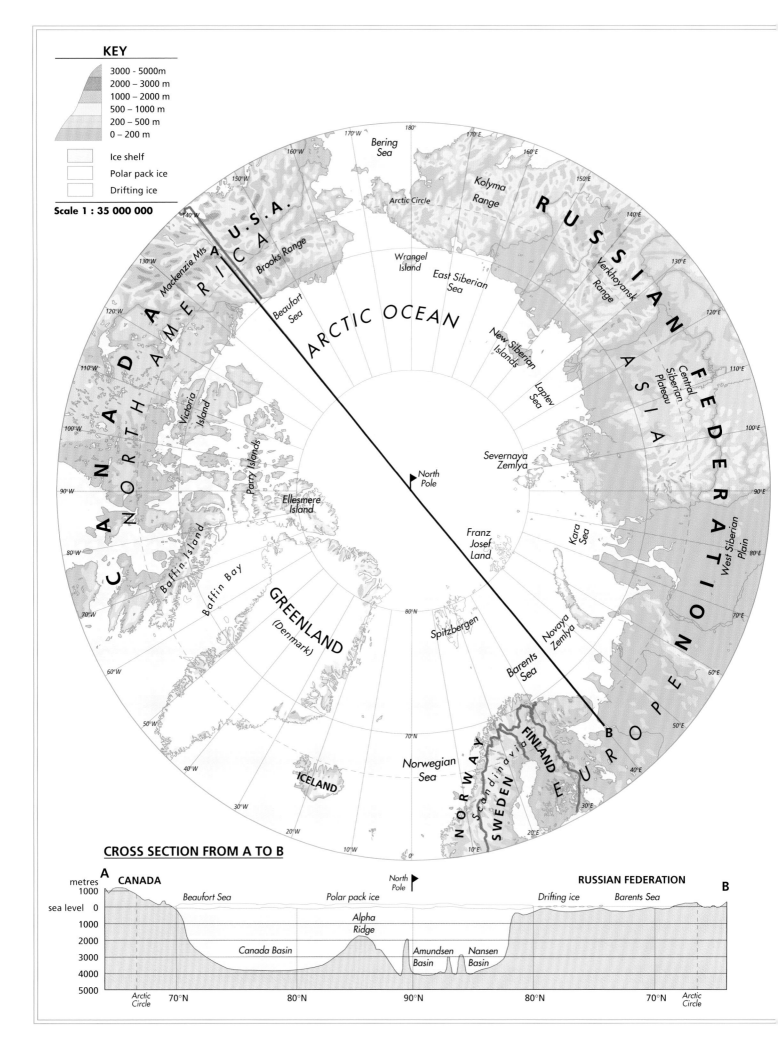

KEY

	3000 – 5000m
	2000 – 3000 m
	1000 – 2000 m
	500 – 1000 m
	200 – 500 m
	0 – 200 m
	Ice shelf
	Polar pack ice
	Drifting ice

Scale 1 : 35 000 000

Bering Sea
Kolyma Range
Arctic Circle
Wrangel Island
East Siberian Sea
Verkhoyansk Range
Brooks Range
Beaufort Sea
ARCTIC OCEAN
New Siberian Islands
Central Siberian Plateau
Mackenzie Mts
U.S.A.
NORTH AMERICA
Laptev Sea
RUSSIAN FEDERATION
ASIA
CANADA
Victoria Island
Parry Islands
Severnaya Zemlya
Ellesmere Island
North Pole
Kara Sea
West Siberian Plain
Franz Josef Land
Baffin Island
Baffin Bay
Spitzbergen
Novaya Zemlya
GREENLAND (Denmark)
Barents Sea
EUROPE
Norwegian Sea
NORWAY
SWEDEN
FINLAND
Scandinavia
ICELAND

CROSS SECTION FROM A TO B

A			North Pole			B
metres	CANADA				RUSSIAN FEDERATION	

1000
sea level 0
1000
2000
3000
4000
5000

Beaufort Sea
Polar pack ice
Drifting ice
Barents Sea
Alpha Ridge
Canada Basin
Amundsen Basin
Nansen Basin
Arctic Circle
70°N
80°N
90°N
80°N
70°N
Arctic Circle

Polar Stereographic projection

MANNED BASES IN THE ANTARCTIC PENINSULA

① Presidente Eduardo Frei Montalva (Chile)
② Comandante Ferraz (Brazil)
③ Capitán Arturo Prat (Chile)
④ Bellingshausen (Russian Federation)
⑤ Teniente Jubany (Argentina)
⑥ Arctowski (Poland)
⑦ General Bernardo O'Higgins (Chile)
⑧ Chang Cheng (Great Wall) (China)
⑨ Artigas (Uruguay)
⑩ General San Martin (Argentina)

KEY

☐	Ice shelf
☐	Ice cap
☐	Polar pack ice
☐	Drifting ice
☐	Glacier

Scale 1 : 35 000 000

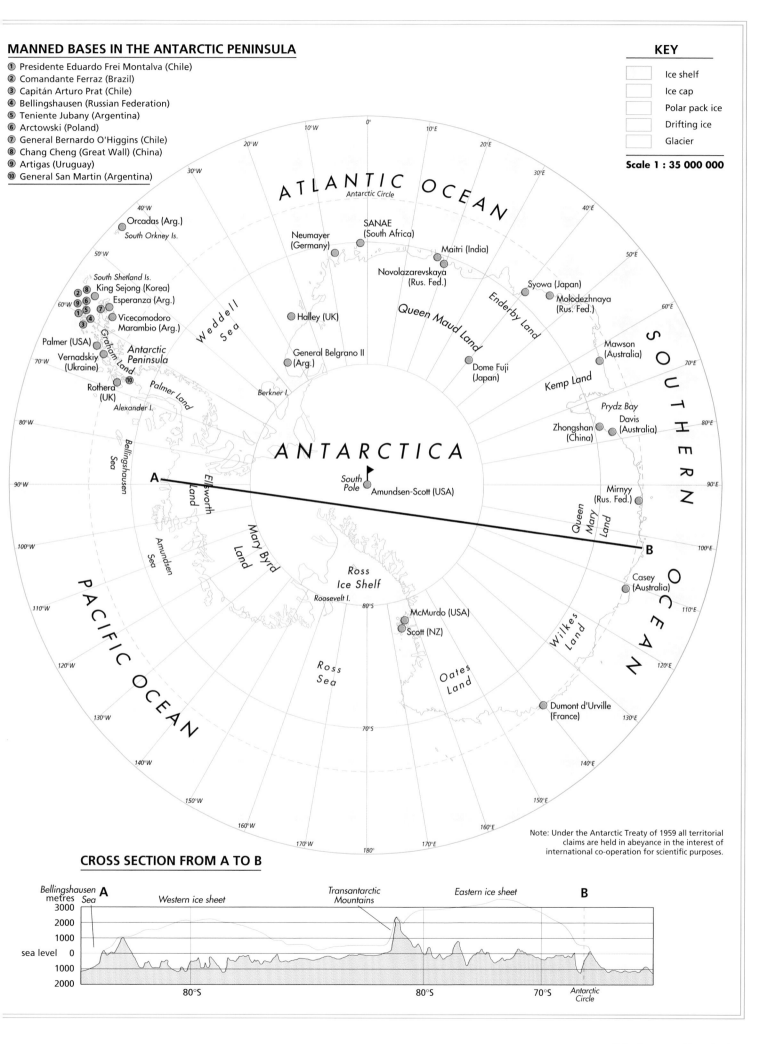

Note: Under the Antarctic Treaty of 1959 all territorial claims are held in abeyance in the interest of international co-operation for scientific purposes.

CROSS SECTION FROM A TO B

Polar Stereographic projection

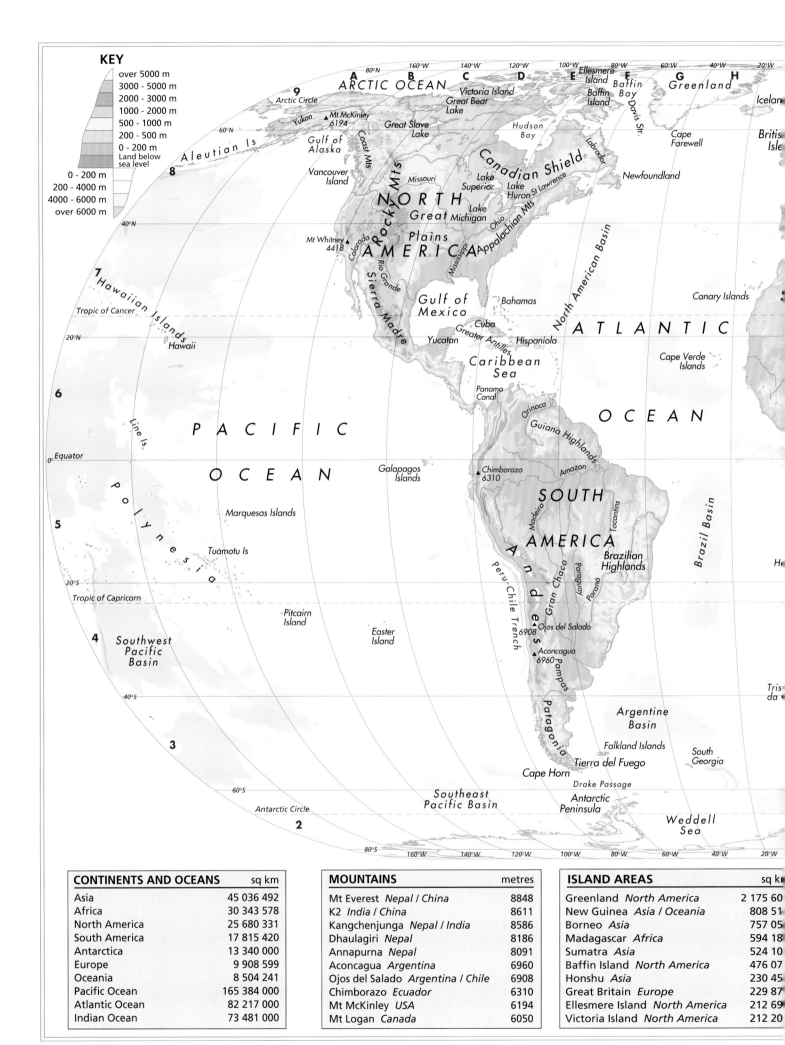

KEY

	over 5000 m
	3000 - 5000 m
	2000 - 3000 m
	1000 - 2000 m
	500 - 1000 m
	200 - 500 m
	0 - 200 m
	Land below sea level

0 - 200 m
200 - 4000 m
4000 - 6000 m
over 6000 m

CONTINENTS AND OCEANS	sq km
Asia	45 036 492
Africa	30 343 578
North America	25 680 331
South America	17 815 420
Antarctica	13 340 000
Europe	9 908 599
Oceania	8 504 241
Pacific Ocean	165 384 000
Atlantic Ocean	82 217 000
Indian Ocean	73 481 000

MOUNTAINS		metres
Mt Everest	Nepal / China	8848
K2	India / China	8611
Kangchenjunga	Nepal / India	8586
Dhaulagiri	Nepal	8186
Annapurna	Nepal	8091
Aconcagua	Argentina	6960
Ojos del Salado	Argentina / Chile	6908
Chimborazo	Ecuador	6310
Mt McKinley	USA	6194
Mt Logan	Canada	6050

ISLAND AREAS		sq k
Greenland	North America	2 175 60
New Guinea	Asia / Oceania	808 51
Borneo	Asia	757 05
Madagascar	Africa	594 18
Sumatra	Asia	524 10
Baffin Island	North America	476 07
Honshu	Asia	230 45
Great Britain	Europe	229 87
Ellesmere Island	North America	212 69
Victoria Island	North America	212 20

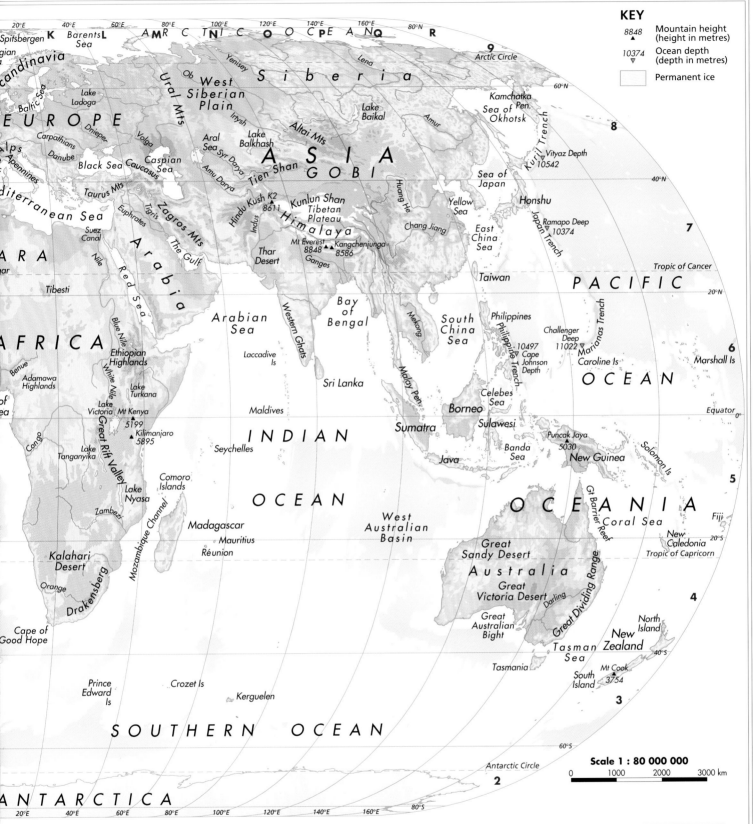

KEY

8848 ▲ Mountain height
(height in metres)

10374 ▽ Ocean depth
(depth in metres)

☐ Permanent ice

Scale 1 : 80 000 000

0   1000   2000   3000 km

Eckert IV projection

LAKES	sq km
Caspian Sea *Asia*	371 000
Lake Superior *North America*	83 270
Lake Victoria *Africa*	68 800
Lake Huron *North America*	60 700
Lake Michigan *North America*	58 020
Aral Sea *Asia*	33 640
Lake Tanganyika *Africa*	32 900
Great Bear Lake *North America*	31 790
Lake Baikal *Asia*	30 500
Great Slave Lake *North America*	28 440

RIVERS	kilometres
Nile *Africa*	6695
Amazon *South America*	6516
Chang Jiang *Asia*	6380
Mississippi-Missouri *North America*	6020
Ob- Irtysh *Asia*	5570
Huang He *Asia*	5464
Congo *Africa*	4667
Mekong *Asia*	4425
Amur *Asia*	4416
Lena *Asia*	4400

WORLD EXTREMES	
Highest Mountain	
Mt Everest *Asia*	8848 m
Largest Inland Water Area	
Caspian Sea	371 000 sq km
Largest Island	
Greenland	2 175 600 sq km
Longest River	
Nile *Africa*	6695 km
Deepest Water	
Marianas Trench *Pacific Ocean*	11 022 m

ABBREVIATIONS OF COUNTRY NAMES

SOUTH AMERICA
FR.G. FRENCH GUIANA
GUY. GUYANA
SUR. SURINAME

AFRICA
B. BURUNDI
BE. BENIN
BUR. BURKINA
CAM. CAMEROON
C.D'I. CÔTE D'IVOIRE
EQ. G. EQUATORIAL
GUINEA
GH. GHANA
R. RWANDA
T. TOGO

EUROPE
A. ANDORRA
ALB. ALBANIA
AUS. AUSTRIA
BEL. BELGIUM
BELA. BELARUS
B.H. BOSNIA-HERZEGOVINA
CR. CROATIA
CYP. CYPRUS
CZ. CZECH REPUBLIC
DEN. DENMARK
EST. ESTONIA
GER. GERMANY
H. HUNGARY
LAT. LATVIA
LITH. LITHUANIA
LUX. LUXEMBOURG

M. MACEDONIA
MO. MOLDOVA
NETH. NETHERLANDS
R.F. RUSSIAN FEDERATION
S. SLOVENIA
SL. SLOVAKIA
SW. SWITZERLAND
YU. YUGOSLAVIA

ASIA
AR. ARMENIA
AZ. AZERBAIJAN
GEO. GEORGIA
IS. ISRAEL
JOR. JORDAN
LEB. LEBANON
U.A.E. UNITED ARAB EMIRATES

TIME COMPARISONS
Time varies around the world due to the earth's rotation causing different parts of the world to be in light or darkness at one time. To account for this, the world is divided into twenty-four Standard Time Zones based on 15° intervals of longitude

1:00am	2:00am	3:00am	4:00am	5:00am	6:00am	7:00am	8:00am	9:00am	10:00am	11:00am	noon
W. Samoa Tonga	Hawaiian Is Cook Is Tahiti	Anchorage Pitcairn I	Vancouver Seattle Los Angeles	Edmonton Phoenix Easter I	Winnipeg Chicago Mexico City	New York Miami Lima	Puerto Rico La Paz Asunción	Nuuk Brasilia Buenos Aires	South Georgia	Azores Cape Verde	Reykja Londo Freeto

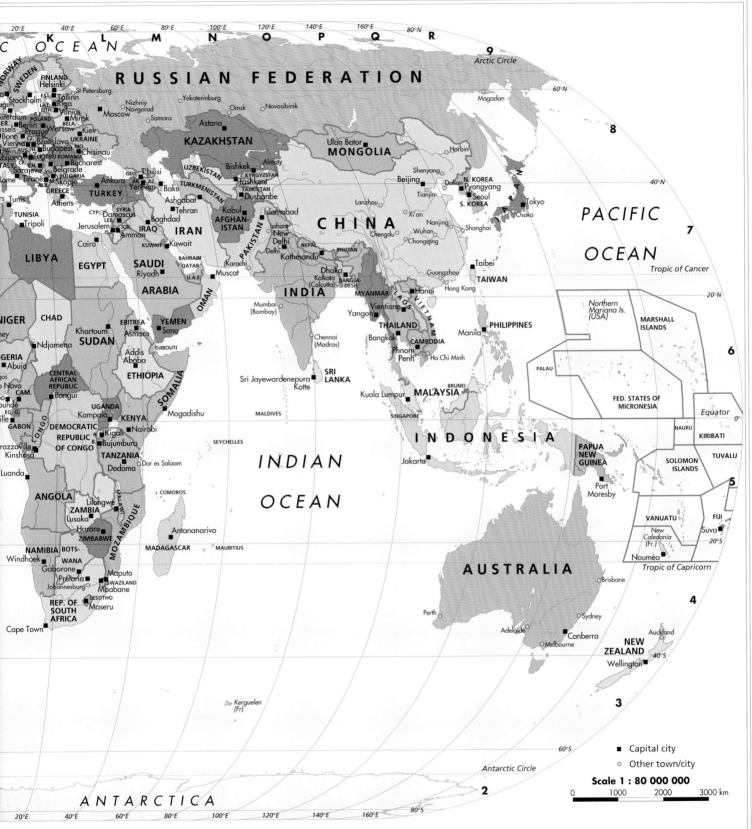

The table below gives examples of times observed at different parts of the world when it is 12 noon in the zone at the Greenwich Meridian 0° longitude). The time at 0° is known as Greenwich Mean Time (GMT).

:00pm	2:00pm	3:00pm	4:00pm	5:00pm	6:00pm	7:00pm	8:00pm	9:00pm	10:00pm	11:00pm	midnight
Oslo Paris nshasa	Helsinki Cairo Cape Town	St Petersburg Riyadh Dodoma	T'bilisi U.A.E. Mauritius	Yekaterinburg Tashkent Karachi	Omsk Almaty Dhaka	Hanoi Bangkok Jakarta	Ulan Bator Hong Kong Perth	Pyongyang Tokyo Palau	Port Moresby Brisbane Canberra	Magadan Solomon Is New Caledonia	Marshall Is Fiji Wellington

Eckert IV projection

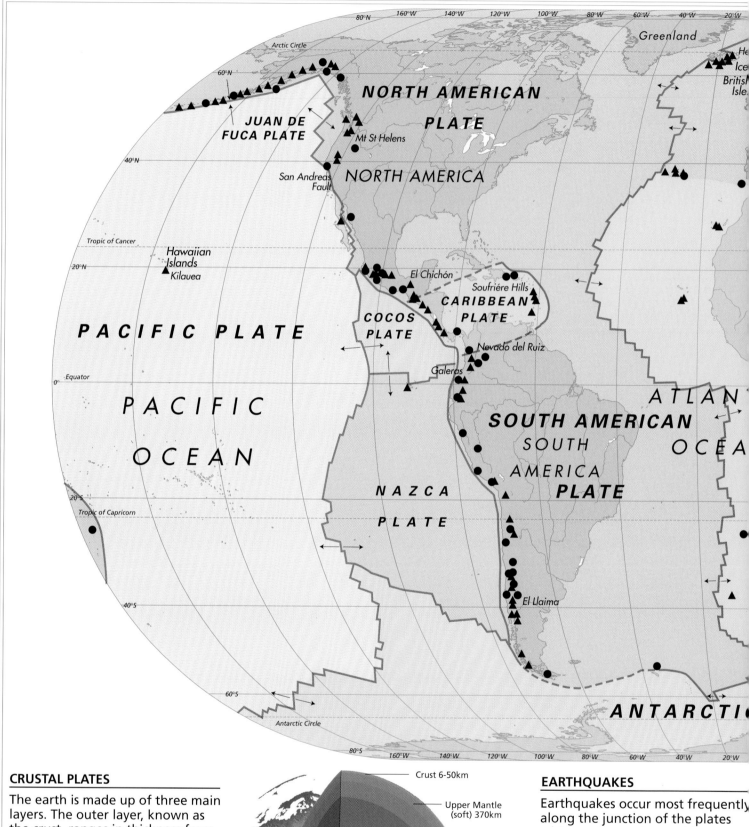

80°N · 160°W · 140°W · 120°W · 100°W · 80°W · 60°W · 40°W · 20°W

Arctic Circle

Greenland

Ice

British
Isles

NORTH AMERICAN

PLATE

60°N

**JUAN DE
FUCA PLATE**

Mt St Helens

40°N

San Andreas
Fault

NORTH AMERICA

Tropic of Cancer

20°N

Hawaiian
Islands
Kilauea

El Chichón

Soufrière Hills

**CARIBBEAN
PLATE**

PACIFIC PLATE

**COCOS
PLATE**

Nevado del Ruiz

0° Equator

Galeras

ATLAN

OCEA

PACIFIC

SOUTH AMERICAN

SOUTH

OCEA

OCEAN

AMERICA PLATE

20°S

NAZCA

Tropic of Capricorn

PLATE

40°S

El Llaima

60°S

ANTARCTI

Antarctic Circle

80°S · 160°W · 140°W · 120°W · 100°W · 80°W · 60°W · 40°W · 20°W

CRUSTAL PLATES

The earth is made up of three main layers. The outer layer, known as the crust, ranges in thickness from a few kilometres under the oceans to almost 50 km under mountain ranges. The middle layer, known as the mantle, makes up 82% of the earth's volume. At the centre (core) of the earth, temperatures reach 4300 °C.

——— Plate boundary

Crust 6-50km

Upper Mantle
(soft) 370km

Transitional
Zone 600km

Lower Mantle
(solid) 1700km

Outer Core
(liquid)
2100km

Inner Core
(solid) 1350km

EARTHQUAKES

Earthquakes occur most frequently along the junction of the plates which make up the earth's crust. They are caused by the release of stress which builds up at the plate edges. When shock waves from these movements reach the surface they are felt as earthquakes which may result in severe damage to property or loss of lives.

● High magnitude earthquake
(over 7.8 on Richter scale)
See page 34 for explanation of Richter scale

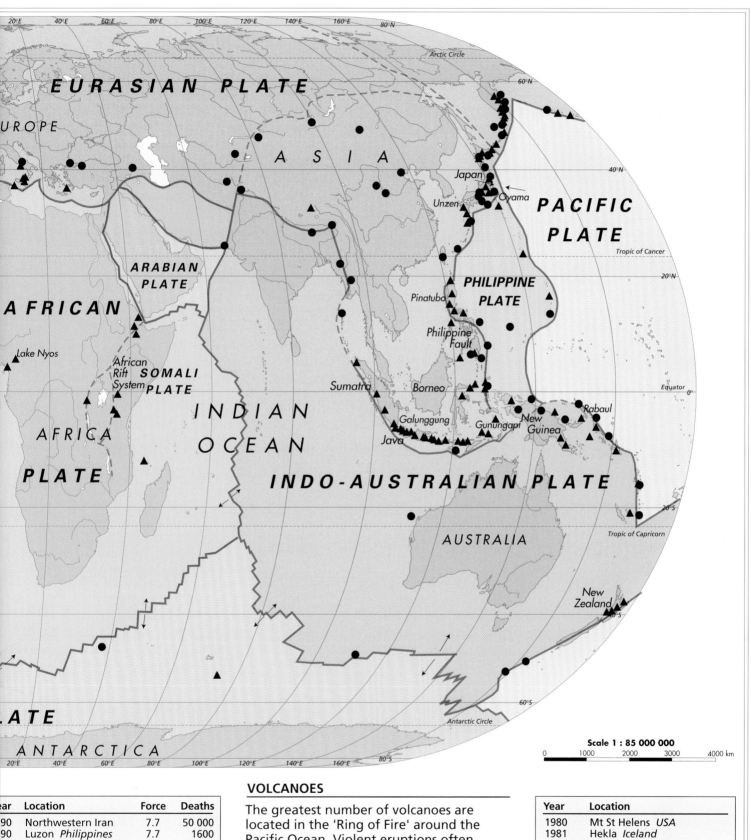

Scale 1 : 85 000 000

0   1000   2000   3000   4000 km

VOLCANOES

The greatest number of volcanoes are located in the 'Ring of Fire' around the Pacific Ocean. Violent eruptions often occur when two plates collide and the heat generated forces molten rock (magma) upwards through weaknesses in the earth's crust. Thousands of volcanic eruptions of varying intensity occur each year.

▲   Active volcano

ear	Location	Force	Deaths
90	Northwestern Iran	7.7	50 000
90	Luzon *Philippines*	7.7	1600
91	Uttar Pradesh *India*	6.1	1600
92	Flores *Indonesia*	7.5	2500
93	Maharashtra *India*	6.4	9700
95	Kobe *Japan*	7.2	5200
95	Sakhalin *Russian Fed*	7.6	2500
97	Quae'n *Iran*	7.1	2400
98	Afghanistan/Tajikistan	6.1,6.9	6300
98	Papua New Guinea	7.1	2180
99	Colombia	6.3	1180
99	Turkey	7.4	15 600
99	Taiwan	7.6	2100
01	El Salvador	7.6	700
01	Gujarat *India*	7.7	30 000

Year	Location
1980	Mt St Helens *USA*
1981	Hekla *Iceland*
1982	El Chichón *Mexico*
1982	Galunggung *Indonesia*
1983	Kilauea *Hawaii*
1983	Oyama *Japan*
1985	Nevado del Ruiz *Colombia*
1986	Lake Nyos *Cameroon*
1991	Pinatubo *Philippines*
1991	Unzen *Japan*
1993	Mayon *Philippines*
1993	Galeras *Colombia*
1994	El Llaima *Chile*
1994	Rabaul *Papua New Guinea*
1997	Soufriére Hills *Montserrat*

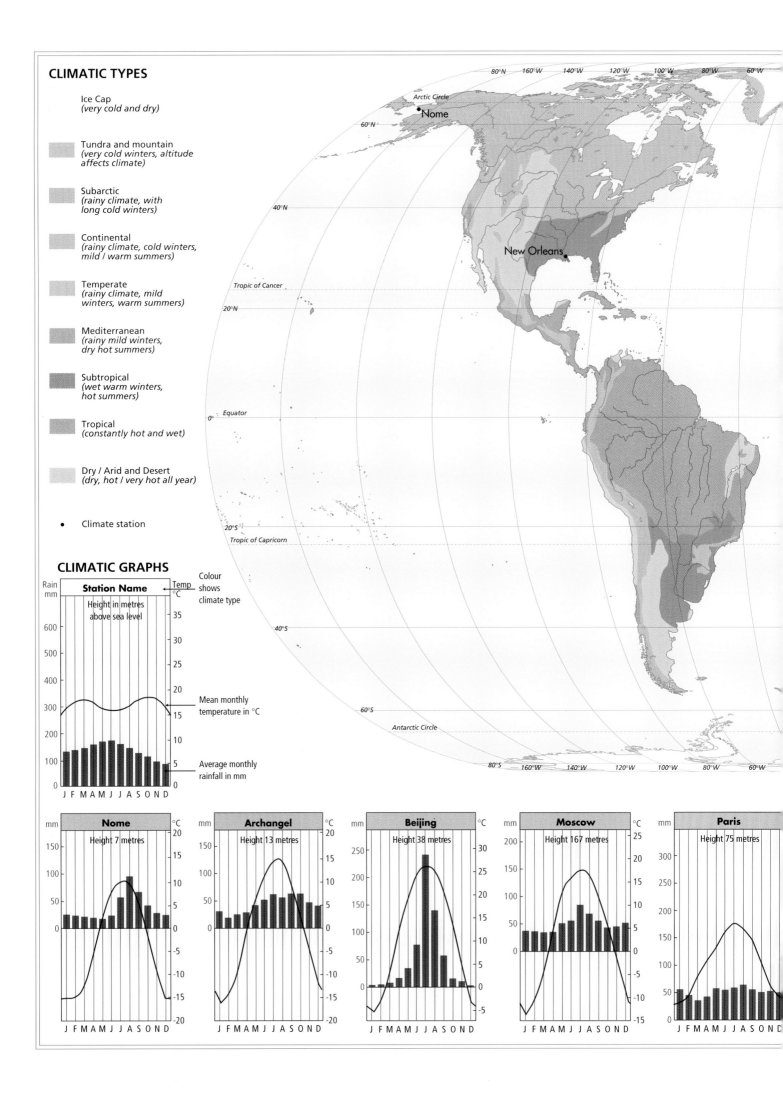

CLIMATIC TYPES

Ice Cap
(very cold and dry)

Tundra and mountain
(very cold winters, altitude affects climate)

Subarctic
(rainy climate, with long cold winters)

Continental
(rainy climate, cold winters, mild / warm summers)

Temperate
(rainy climate, mild winters, warm summers)

Mediterranean
(rainy mild winters, dry hot summers)

Subtropical
(wet warm winters, hot summers)

Tropical
(constantly hot and wet)

Dry / Arid and Desert
(dry, hot / very hot all year)

• Climate station

CLIMATIC GRAPHS

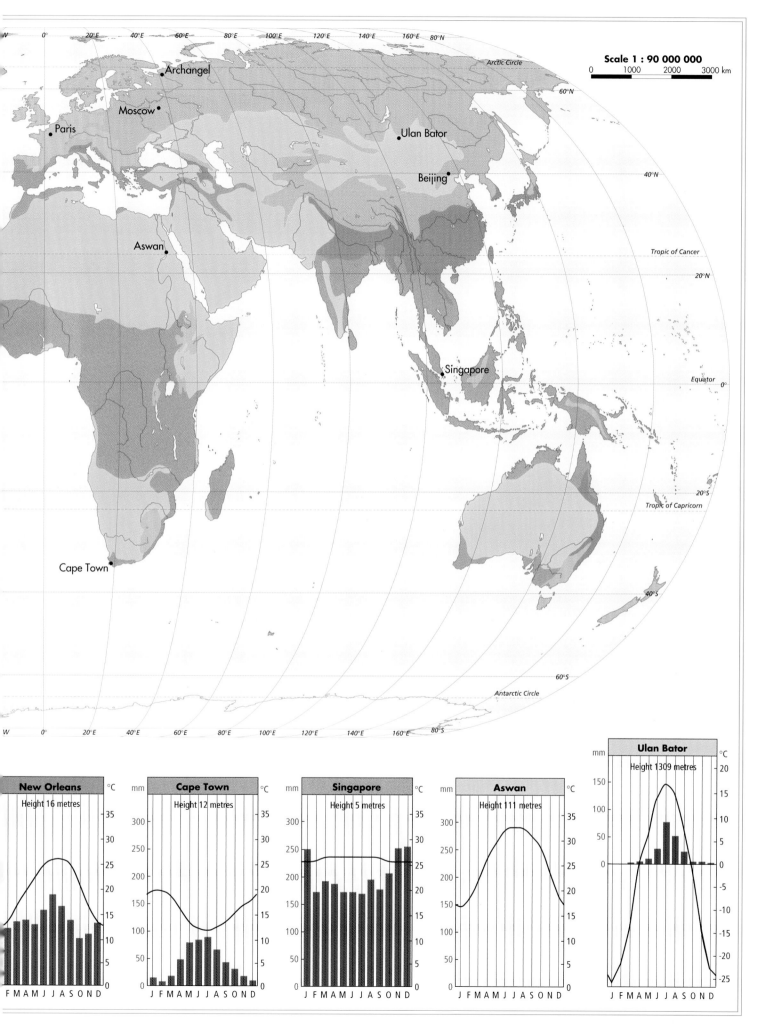

Scale 1 : 90 000 000

0   1000   2000   3000 km

Archangel

Moscow

Paris

Ulan Bator

Beijing

Aswan

Arctic Circle

60°N

40°N

Tropic of Cancer

20°N

Singapore

Equator   0°

20°S

Tropic of Capricorn

Cape Town

40°S

60°S

Antarctic Circle

80°S

0°   20°E   40°E   60°E   80°E   100°E   120°E   140°E   160°E   80°N

Eckert IV projection

New Orleans
Height 16 metres
°C

Cape Town
Height 12 metres
mm   °C

Singapore
Height 5 metres
mm   °C

Aswan
Height 111 metres
mm   °C

Ulan Bator
Height 1309 metres
mm   °C

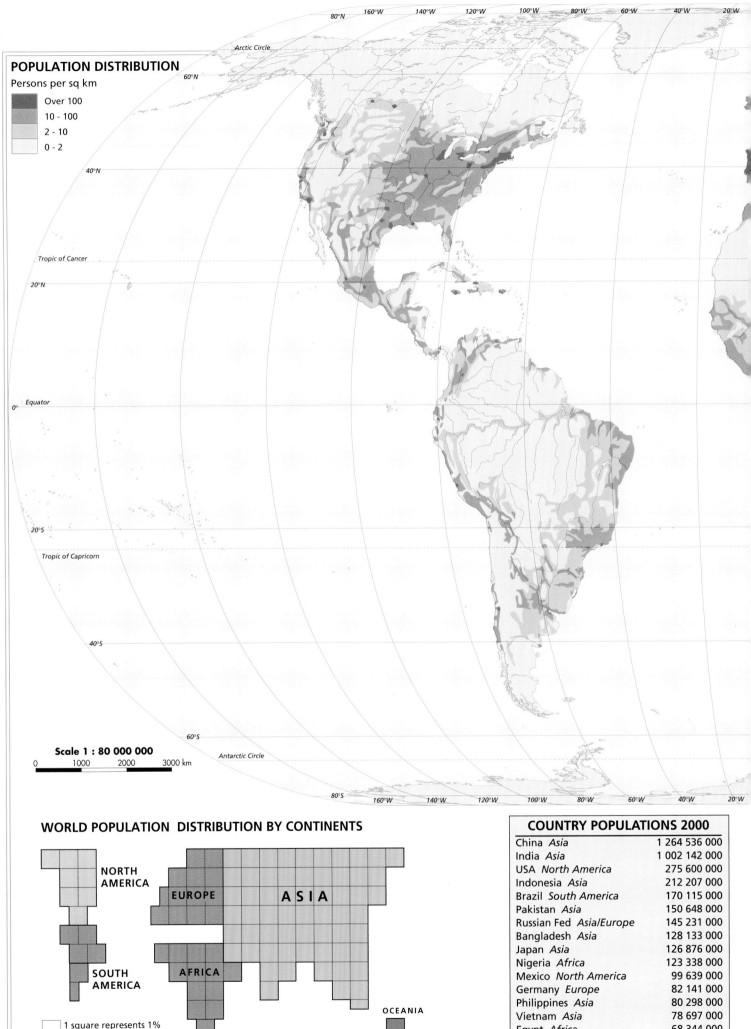

POPULATION DISTRIBUTION

Persons per sq km

- Over 100
- 10 - 100
- 2 - 10
- 0 - 2

Arctic Circle

80°N

60°N

40°N

Tropic of Cancer

20°N

0° Equator

20°S

Tropic of Capricorn

40°S

60°S

Antarctic Circle

80°S

160°W 140°W 120°W 100°W 80°W 60°W 40°W 20°W

Scale 1 : 80 000 000

0 1000 2000 3000 km

WORLD POPULATION DISTRIBUTION BY CONTINENTS

NORTH AMERICA

EUROPE

ASIA

SOUTH AMERICA

AFRICA

OCEANIA

1 square represents 1% of total world population

COUNTRY POPULATIONS 2000

China *Asia*	1 264 536 000
India *Asia*	1 002 142 000
USA *North America*	275 600 000
Indonesia *Asia*	212 207 000
Brazil *South America*	170 115 000
Pakistan *Asia*	150 648 000
Russian Fed *Asia/Europe*	145 231 000
Bangladesh *Asia*	128 133 000
Japan *Asia*	126 876 000
Nigeria *Africa*	123 338 000
Mexico *North America*	99 639 000
Germany *Europe*	82 141 000
Philippines *Asia*	80 298 000
Vietnam *Asia*	78 697 000
Egypt *Africa*	68 344 000

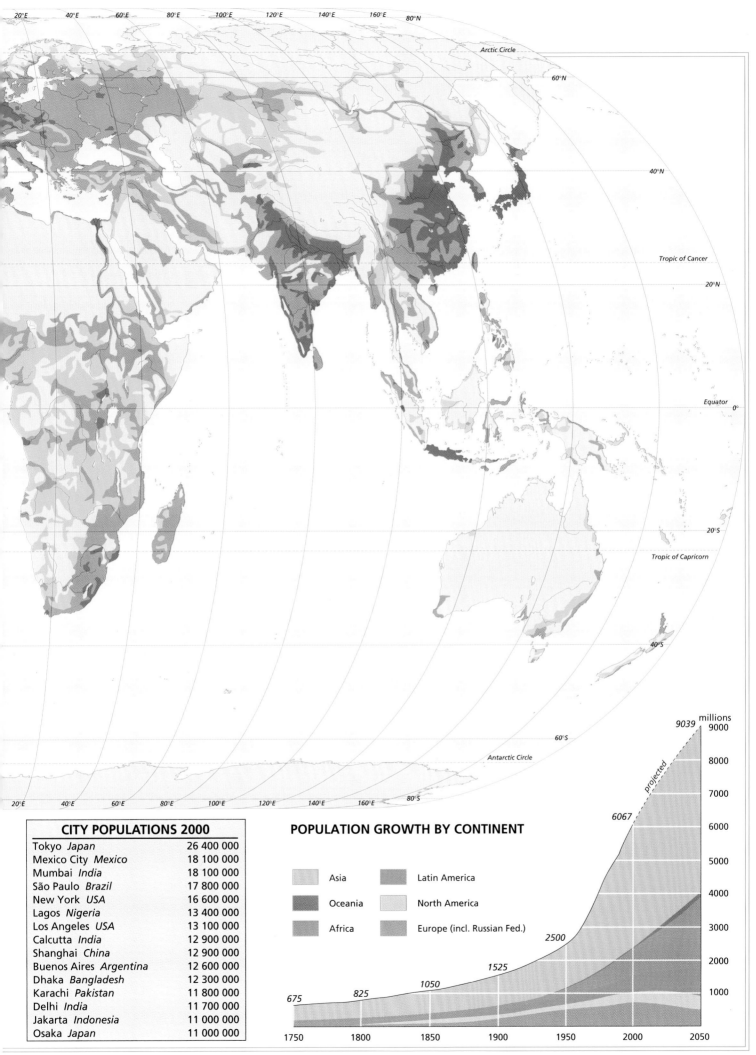

CITY POPULATIONS 2000	
Tokyo *Japan*	26 400 000
Mexico City *Mexico*	18 100 000
Mumbai *India*	18 100 000
São Paulo *Brazil*	17 800 000
New York *USA*	16 600 000
Lagos *Nigeria*	13 400 000
Los Angeles *USA*	13 100 000
Calcutta *India*	12 900 000
Shanghai *China*	12 900 000
Buenos Aires *Argentina*	12 600 000
Dhaka *Bangladesh*	12 300 000
Karachi *Pakistan*	11 800 000
Delhi *India*	11 700 000
Jakarta *Indonesia*	11 000 000
Osaka *Japan*	11 000 000

POPULATION GROWTH BY CONTINENT

Asia
Oceania
Africa
Latin America
North America
Europe (incl. Russian Fed.)

Eckert IV projection

The important names on the reference maps in the atlas are found in the index. The names are listed in alphabetical order. Each entry gives the country or region of the world in which the name is located followed by the page number, its alphanumeric grid reference and then its co-ordinates of latitude and longitude. Names of very large areas may have these co-ordinates omitted. Area names which are included in the index are referenced to the centre of the feature. In the case of rivers, the mouth or confluence is taken as the point of reference. It is therefore necessary to follow the river upstream from this point to find its name on the map.

On the map of part of Ireland to the right Dublin is found in grid square C3 at latitude 53° 21'N longitude 6° 18'W.

This appears in the index as **Dublin** Rep. of Ire. **11 C3** 53.21N 6.18W. The chart below explains all the elements listed for each entry.

Dublin	Rep. of Ireland	**11**	**C3**	53.21N	6.18W
Name of the feature to be located.	Name of the country in which the feature is situated.	Page in the atlas where the feature is shown on the largest scale.	Grid square where the feature is found.	Degrees and minutes north or south of the equator.	Degrees and minutes east or west of Greenwich meridian.

Sometimes an abbreviated description of a feature is included in the entry. A list of abbreviations used in the index is included below.

Abbreviations

Afghan.	Afghanistan	Equat. Guinea	Equatorial Guinea	Neth.	Netherlands
Austa.	Australasia	*est.*	estuary	Neth. Ant.	Netherlands Antilles
b., **B.**	bay, Bay	*f.*	physical feature eg. valley, plain	N. Korea	North Korea
Bangla.	Bangladesh			Oc.	Ocean
Bosnia.	Bosnia-Herzegovina	**G.**	Gulf	*pen.*, **Pen.**	peninsula, Peninsula
c., **C.**	cape, Cape	I.o.M	Isle of Man	Phil.	Philippines
C. America	Central America	*l.* **L.**	lake, Lake	P.N.G.	Papua New Guinea
C.A.R.	Central African Republic	Lux.	Luxembourg	*r.*	river
d.	Internal division eg. state, county	**Mt.**	Mount	Rep. of Ire.	Republic of Ireland
		mtn.	mountain	**Resr.**	Reservoir
des.	desert	*mts.*, Mts.	mountains	R.S.A.	Republic of South Africa

Russian Fed.	Russian Federation
S. America	South America
S. Korea	South Korea
str., **Str.**	strait, Strait
Switz.	Switzerland
U.K.	United Kingdom
U.S.A.	United States of America
W. Sahara	Western Sahara
Yugo.	Yugoslavia

A

Aberdeen Scotland **10 E5** 57.08N 2.07W
Aberystwyth Wales **11 D3** 52.25N 4.06W
Abidjan Côte d'Ivoire **40 C5** 5.19N 4.01W
Abuja Nigeria **40 D5** 9.12N 7.11E
Acapulco Mexico **51 G3** 16.51N 99.56W
Accra Ghana **40 C5** 5.33N 0.15W
Aconcagua *mtn.* Argentina **55 D3** 32.37S 70.00W
Adamawa Highlands Nigeria/Cameroon **40 E5** 7.05N 12.00E
Adana Turkey **19 D2** 37.00N 35.19E
Addis Ababa Ethiopia **40 G5** 9.03N 38.42E
Adelaide Australia **64 D2** 34.56S 138.36E
Aden, G of Indian Ocean **28 D2** 13.00N 50.00E
Adriatic Sea Med. Sea **20 F5** 42.30N 16.00E
Aegean Sea Med. Sea **18 F2** 39.00N 25.00E
Afghanistan Asia **28 F4** 33.00N 65.30E
Africa 40
Ahmadabad India **29 G3** 23.03N 72.40E
Alausí Ecuador **54 D6** 2.00S 78.50W
Albania Europe **18 E3** 41.00N 20.00E
Alexandria Egypt **40 F8** 31.13N 29.55E
Algeria Africa **40 C7** 28.00N 2.00E
Algiers Algeria **40 D8** 36.50N 3.00E
Alice Springs Australia **64 D3** 23.42S 133.52E
Allier *r.* France **18 D3** 46.58N 3.04E
Alps *mts.* Europe **18 D3** 46.00N 7.30E
Altai Mts. Mongolia **30 B8** 46.30N 93.30E
Altiplano *f.* Bolivia **56 B3** 18.00S 67.30W
Amazon *r.* Brazil **56 C4** 2.00S 50.00W
Amazon Delta *f.* Brazil **56 C5** 0.00 50.00W
Amman Jordan **28 C4** 31.57N 35.56E
Amsterdam Neth. **18 D4** 52.22N 4.54E
Amur *r.* Russian Fed. **26 D7** 53.17N 140.00E
Anápolis Brazil **56 D3** 16.19S 48.58W
Anchorage U.S.A. **50 D6** 61.10N 150.00W
Andaman Is. India **29 I2** 12.00N 93.00E
Andaman Sea Indian Oc. **29 I2** 11.00N 96.00E
Andes *mts.* S. America **54 D6** 15.00S 74.00W
Andorra Europe **18 D3** 42.30N 1.32E
Angola Africa **40 E3** 12.00S 18.00E
Ankara Turkey **19 G2** 39.55N 32.50E
Anshan China **30 E8** 41.05N 122.58E
Antananarivo Madagascar **41 H3** 18.52S 47.30E
Antarctica 67
Antigua and Barbuda Leeward Is. **54 E8** 17.30N 61.49W
Antofagasta Chile **55 D4** 23.40S 70.23W

Apennines *mts.* Italy **20 C6** 44.00N 11.00E
Appalachian Mts. U.S.A. **50 H4** 39.30N 78.00W
Arabian Sea Asia **28 F3** 19.00N 65.00E
Arafura Sea Austa. **64 D5** 9.00S 135.00E
Araguaína Brazil **56 D4** 7.16S 48.18W
Araguari Brazil **56 D4** 18.38S 48.13W
Aral Sea Asia **28 E5** 45.00N 60.00E
Archangel Russian Fed. **19 H5** 64.32N 41.10E
Arctic Ocean 66
Arequipa Peru **56 A3** 16.25S 71.32W
Argentina S. America **55 E3** 35.00S 65.00W
Argentino, L. Argentina **55 D1** 50.15S 72.25W
Arica Chile **54 D5** 18.30S 70.20W
Arkansas *r.* U.S.A. **51 G4** 33.50N 91.00W
Armenia Asia **28 D5** 40.00N 45.00E
Arnhem Land *f.* Australia **64 D4** 13.00S 132.30E
Aruba *i.* Neth. Ant. **54 D8** 12.30N 70.00W
Arusha Tanzania **40 G4** 3.21S 36.40E
Ashford England **11 G2** 51.08N 0.53E
Asia 26 - 27
Asmara Eritrea **40 G6** 15.20N 38.58E
Asunción Paraguay **56 C2** 25.15S 57.40W
Atacama Desert S. America **55 D4** 20.00S 69.00W
Athens Greece **18 F2** 37.59N 23.42E
Atlanta U.S.A. **51 H4** 33.45N 84.23W
Atlas Mts. Africa **40 C8** 33.00N 4.00W
Auckland New Zealand **65 H2** 36.52S 174.45E
Australia Austa. **64 D3** 25.00S 135.00E
Austria Europe **18 E3** 47.30N 14.00E
Ayacucho Peru **54 D5** 13.10S 74.15W
Ayers Rock *hill* Australia **64 D3** 25.20S 131.00E
Ayr Scotland **10 D4** 55.28N 4.37W
Azerbaijan Asia **28 D5** 40.10N 47.50E
Azov, Sea of Ukraine **19 G3** 46.00N 36.30E

B

Baffin B. Canada **50 I6** 74.00N 70.00W
Baffin I. Canada **50 H6** 68.50N 70.00W
Baghdad Iraq **28 D4** 33.20N 44.26E
Bahrain Asia **28 E3** 26.00N 50.35E
Baikal, L. Russian Fed. **30 C9** 53.30N 108.00E
Baku Azerbaijan **28 D5** 40.22N 49.53E
Balbina Resr. Brazil **56 C4** 1.30S 60.00W
Balearic Is. Spain **18 D2** 39.30N 2.30E
Balkan Mts. Bulgaria **18 F3** 42.50N 24.30E
Balkhash Kazakstan **26 J7** 46.51N 75.00E
Baltic Sea Europe **18 E4** 56.30N 19.00E

Baltimore U.S.A. **51 H4** 39.18N 76.38W
Bamako Mali **40 C6** 12.40N 7.59W
Bandar Seri Begawan Brunei **31 D4** 4.56N 114.58E
Bangkok Thailand **31 C5** 13.45N 100.35E
Bangladesh Asia **29 H3** 24.00N 90.00E
Bangui C.A.R. **40 E5** 4.23N 18.37E
Baotou China **30 C8** 40.38N 109.59E
Barbados Lesser Antilles **54 F8** 13.20N 59.40W
Barcelona Spain **18 D3** 41.25N 2.10E
Barents Sea Arctic Ocean **26 E10** 73.00N 40.00E
Barinas Venezuela **54 D7** 8.36N 70.15W
Barranquilla Colombia **54 D8** 11.00N 74.50W
Basel Switz. **18 D3** 47.33N 7.36E
Bass Str. Australia **64 E2** 39.45S 146.00E
Bath England **11 E2** 51.22N 2.22W
Beijing China **30 D7** 39.55N 116.25E
Beirut Lebanon **24 C4** 33.52N 35.30E
Belarus Europe **18 F4** 53.00N 28.00E
Belém Brazil **56 D4** 1.27S 48.29W
Belfast N. Ireland **11 D4** 54.36N 5.57W
Belgium Europe **18 D4** 51.00N 4.30E
Belgrade Yugo. **18 F3** 44.49N 20.28E
Belize C. America **51 H3** 17.00N 88.30W
Belmopan Belize **51 H3** 17.25N 88.46W
Belo Horizonte Brazil **57 D3** 19.45S 43.53W
Bengal, B. of Indian Ocean **29 H2** 17.00N 89.00E
Benin Africa **40 D5** 9.00N 2.30E
Benin, Bight of Africa **38 E6** 5.30N 3.00E
Ben Nevis *mtn.* Scotland **10 D5** 56.48N 5.00W
Bergen Norway **18 D5** 60.23N 5.20E
Bering Sea N. America/Asia **27 T8** 60.00N 170.00E
Berlin Germany **18 E4** 52.32N 13.25E
Bermuda *i.* Atlantic Oc. **50 I4** 32.18N 65.00W
Berne Switz. **18 D3** 46.57N 7.26E
Berwick-upon-Tweed England **10 E4** 55.46N 2.00W
Bhutan Asia **29 H3** 27.25N 90.00E
Bié Plateau *f.* Angola **41 E3** 13.00S 16.00E
Birmingham England **11 F3** 52.30N 1.55W
Biscay, B. of France **18 C3** 45.30N 3.00W
Bissau Guinea Bissau **40 B6** 11.52N 15.39W
Blackburn England **11 E3** 53.44N 2.30W
Blackpool England **11 E3** 53.48N 3.03W
Black Sea Europe **19 G3** 43.00N 35.00E
Blanc, Mont *mtn.* Europe **18 D3** 45.50N 6.52E
Bogotá Colombia **54 D7** 4.38N 74.05W
Bolivia S. America **56 B3** 17.00S 65.00W
Bologna Italy **20 D6** 44.30N 11.20E

Bolton England **11 E3** 53.35N 2.26W
Bombay *see* **Mumbai** India **29**
Bonn Germany **18 D4** 50.44N 7.06E
Bordeaux France **18 C3** 44.50N 0.34W
Borneo *i.* Asia **31 D4** 1.00N 114.00E
Bosnia-Herzegovina Europe **18 E3** 44.00N 18.00E
Boston U.S.A. **50 I4** 42.15N 71.05W
Bothnia, G. of Europe **18 E5** 63.30N 20.30E
Botswana Africa **41 F2** 22.00S 24.00E
Bournemouth England **11 F2** 50.43N 1.53W
Bradford England **11 F3** 53.47N 1.45W
Brahmaputra *r.* Asia **29 I3** 23.50N 89.45E
Brasília Brazil **56 D3** 15.54S 47.50W
Bratislava Slovakia **18 E3** 48.10N 17.10E
Brazil S. America **56 C4** 10.00S 52.00W
Brazilian Highlands Brazil **56 D3** 17.00S 48.00W
Brazzaville Congo **40 E4** 4.14S 15.14E
Brighton England **11 F2** 50.50N 0.09W
Brisbane Australia **64 F3** 27.30S 153.00E
Bristol England **11 E2** 51.26N 2.35W
Bristol Channel England/Wales **11 D2** 51.17N 3.20W
British Isles Europe **16 C4** 54.00N 5.00W
Brunei Asia **31 D4** 4.56N 114.58E
Brussels Belgium **18 D4** 50.50N 4.23E
Bucharest Romania **18 F3** 44.25N 26.06E
Budapest Hungary **18 E3** 47.30N 19.03E
Buenos Aires Argentina **55 F3** 34.40S 58.30W
Bujumbura Burundi **40 F4** 3.22S 29.21E
Bulgaria Europe **18 F3** 42.30N 25.00E
Burkina Africa **40 C6** 12.15N 1.30W
Burma *see* **Myanmar** Asia **29**
Bursa Turkey **19 F3** 40.11N 29.04E
Burundi Africa **40 G4** 3.30S 30.00E

C

Caernarfon Wales **11 D3** 53.08N 4.17W
Cagliari Italy **20 C3** 39.14N 9.07E
Cairns Australia **64 E4** 16.51S 145.43E
Cairo Egypt **40 G8** 30.03N 31.15E
Calais France **18 D4** 50.57N 1.50E
Calcutta India **29 H3** 22.35N 88.21E
Calgary Canada **50 F5** 51.05N 114.05W
Cali Colombia **54 D7** 3.24N 76.30W
California, G. of Mexico **51 F5** 28.30N 112.30W
Cambodia Asia **31 C5** 12.00N 105.00E
Cambrian Mts. Wales **11 E3** 52.33N 3.33W

ıbridge England **11 G3** 52.13N 0.08E
ıeroon Africa **40 E5** 6.00N 12.30E
ıeroun, Mt. Cameroon **40 D5** 4.20N 9.05E
ıpeche B. Mexico **51 G3** 19.30N 94.00W
ıpinas Brazil **57 D2** 22.54S 47.06W
ada N. America **50 F6** 60.00N 105.00W
adian Shield *f.* N. America **50 G5** 50.00N 0.00W
ary Is. Atlantic Oc. **40 B7** 29.00N 15.00W
averal, C. U.S.A. **51 H3** 28.28N 80.28W
berra Australia **64 E2** 35.18S 149.08E
tabrian Mts. Spain **18 C3** 43.00N 6.00W
e Breton I. Canada **50 I5** 46.00N 61.00W
e Town R.S.A. **41 E1** 33.56S 18.28E
e York Pen. Australia **64 E4** 12.40S 142.20E
acas Venezuela **54 E8** 10.35N 66.56W
diff Wales **11 E2** 51.28N 3.11W
digan B. Wales **11 D3** 52.30N 4.30W
ibbean Sea C. America **51 H3** 15.00N 75.00W
isle England **11 E4** 54.54N 2.55W
pathian Mts. Europe **50 F3** 48.45N 23.45E
pentaria, G. of Australia **64 D4** 14.00S 140.00E
rauntuohill *mts.* Rep. of Ire. **11 B2** 52.00N .45W
cade Range *mts.* U.S.A. **48 K7** 44.00N 21.30W
pian Sea Asia **28 D5** 42.00N 51.00E
casus *mts.* Europe **28 B5** 43.00N 44.00E
enne French Guiana **54 F7** 4.55N 52.18W
ebes Sea Indonesia **31 E4** 3.00N 122.00E
tral African Republic Africa **40 E5** 6.30N 0.00E
d Africa **40 E6** 13.00N 19.00E
d, L. Africa **40 E6** 13.30N 14.00E
ngchun China **30 E8** 43.50N 125.20E
ng Jiang *r.* China **30 D7** 31.40N 121.15E
ngsha China **30 D6** 28.10N 113.00E
nnel Is. U.K. **18 C3** 49.28N 2.13W
ngdu China **30 C7** 30.37N 104.06E
rbourg France **11 F1** 49.38N 1.37W
ster England **11 E3** 53.12N 2.53W
viot Hills U.K. **10 E4** 55.22N 2.24W
cago U.S.A. **50 H4** 41.50N 87.45W
le S. America **55 D2** 33.00S 71.00W
tern Hills England **8 F1** 51.40N 0.53W
na Asia **30 C7** 33.00N 103.00E
sinau Moldova **19 F3** 47.00N 28.50E
ongqing China **30 C6** 29.31N 106.35E
istchurch New Zealand **65 H1** 43.32S 172.37E
cinnati U.S.A. **51 H4** 39.10N 84.30W
de *r.* Scotland **10 E4** 55.58N 4.53W
l, C, U.S.A. **50 I4** 42.08N 70.10W
ombia S. America **54 D7** 5.00N 75.00W
ombo Sri Lanka **29 G1** 6.55N 79.52E
orado *r.* U.S.A./Mexico **50 F4** 31.45N 114.40W
umbus Ohio U.S.A. **50 H4** 39.59N 83.03W
mo, L. Italy **20 C7** 46.05N 9.17E
moros Africa **40 H3** 12.15S 44.00E
nakry Guinea **40 B5** 9.30N 13.43W
ncepción Chile **55 D3** 36.50S 73.03W
ngo Africa **40 E4** 1.00S 16.00E
ngo *r.* Africa **40 E4** 6.00S 12.30E
ok, Mt. New Zealand **65 H1** 43.36S 170.09E
oper Creek *r.* Australia **64 E3** 28.33S 137.46E
oenhagen Denmark **18 E5** 55.43N 12.34E
al Sea Pacific Oc. **64 F4** 13.00S 150.00E
doba Argentina **55 E3** 31.25S 64.11W
k Rep. of Ire. **18 C4** 51.54N 8.28W
rib, Lough Rep. of Ire. **11 B3** 53.26N 9.14W
sica *i.* France **18 D3** 42.00N 9.10E
sta Rica C. America **70 E6** 10.00N 84.00W
e d'Ivoire Africa **40 C5** 7.00N 5.30W
swold Hills England **11 E2** 51.50N 2.00W
ventry England **11 F3** 52.25N 1.31W
wley England **11 F2** 51.07N 0.10W
te *i.* Greece **18 F2** 35.15N 25.00E
we England **11 E3** 53.06N 2.28W
atia Europe **18 E3** 45.30N 17.00E
ydon England **11 F2** 51.23N 0.06W
oa C. America **51 H3** 22.00N 79.00W
itiba Brazil **56 D2** 25.24S 49.16W
orus Asia **19 G2** 35.00N 33.00E
ech Republic Europe **18 E3** 49.30N 15.00E

kar Senegal **40 B6** 14.38N 17.27W
ian China **30 E7** 38.53N 121.37E
las U.S.A. **51 G4** 32.47N 96.48W
mascus Syria **28 C4** 33.30N 36.19E
Nang Vietnam **31 C5** 16.04N 108.14E
nube *r.* Europe **18 F3** 45.26N 29.38E
es Salaam Tanzania **40 G4** 6.51S 39.18E
ling *r.* Australia **64 E2** 34.05S 141.57E
lington England **11 F4** 54.33N 1.33W
win Australia **64 D4** 12.23S 130.44E
vis Str. N. America **50 J6** 66.00N 58.00W
ad Sea Jordan **28 C4** 31.25N 35.30E
Democratic Republic of Congo Africa **40 F4** 2.00S 22.00E
Deccan *f.* India **29 G2** 18.00N 76.30E
Denmark Europe **18 D4** 56.00N 9.00E
Denver U.S.A. **50 G4** 39.45N 104.58W
Derby England **11 F3** 52.55N 1.28W
Detroit U.S.A. **50 H4** 42.23N 83.05W
Dhaka Bangla. **29 I3** 23.42N 90.22E
Dieppe France **9 G1** 49.55N 1.05E
Dijon France **18 D3** 47.20N 5.02E
Dinaric Alps *mts.* Bosnia./Croatia **18 E3** 44.00N 16.30E
Djibouti Africa **40 H6** 12.00N 42.50E
Djibouti *town* Djibouti **40 H6** 11.35N 43.11E
Dnieper *r.* Europe **19 G4** 46.30N 32.25E
Dniestr *r.* Europe **18 F3** 46.21N 30.20E
Dniprodzerzhyns'k Ukraine **18 F3** 48.30N 34.37E
Dnipropetrovs'k Ukraine **19 G3** 48.29N 35.00E
Dodecanese *is.* Greece **18 F2** 37.00N 27.00E
Dodoma Tanzania **40 G4** 6.10S 35.40E
Dolomites *mts.* Italy **20 D7** 46.25N 11.50E
Dominica Windward Is. **54 E8** 15.30N 61.30W
Dominican Republic C. America **51 I3** 18.00N 70.00W
Doncaster England **11 F3** 53.31N 1.09W
Donets'k Ukraine **19 G3** 48.00N 37.50E
Dore, Mont *mtn.* France **18 D3** 45.32N 2.49E
Dornoch Firth *est.* Scotland **10 E5** 57.50N 4.04W
Dortmund Germany **18 D4** 51.32N 7.27E
Douala Cameroon **40 D5** 4.05N 9.43E
Douglas I.o.M. **11 D4** 54.09N 4.29W
Dover England **11 G2** 51.07N 1.19E
Drakensberg *mts.* R.S.A. **41 F1** 30.00S 29.00E
Dresden Germany **18 E4** 51.03N 13.45E
Drogheda Rep. of Ire. **11 C3** 53.43N 6.23W
Dublin Rep. of Ire. **11 C3** 53.21N 6.18W
Duluth U.S.A. **50 G5** 46.50N 92.10W
Dumfries Scotland **11 E4** 55.04N 3.37W
Dundalk Rep. of Ire. **11 C4** 54.01N 6.24W
Dundee Scotland **10 E5** 56.28N 3.00W
Dunedin New Zealand **65 H1** 45.53S 170.31E
Durban R.S.A. **41 G1** 29.53S 31.00E
Durham England **11 F4** 54.47N 1.34W
Dushanbe Tajikistan **29 F4** 38.38N 68.51E
Düsseldorf Germany **18 D4** 51.13N 6.47E

E

Eastbourne England **11 G2** 50.46N 0.18E
East China Sea Asia **30 E6** 29.00N 125.00E
Eastern Ghats *mts.* India **29 G2** 16.30N 80.30E
East London R.S.A. **41 F1** 33.00S 27.54E
Ecuador S. America **54 D6** 2.00S 78.00W
Edinburgh Scotland **10 E4** 55.57N 3.13W
Edmonton Canada **50 F5** 53.34N 113.25W
Edwards Plateau *f.* U.S.A. **51 G4** 30.30N 100.30W
Egypt Africa **40 F7** 26.30N 29.30E
Eighty Mile Beach *f.* Australia **64 C4** 19.00S 121.00E
Elbe *r.* Germany **18 E4** 53.33N 10.00E
El Gîza Egypt **40 G7** 30.01N 31.12E
Elgon, Mt. Kenya/Uganda **42 A3** 1.07N 34.35E
Ellesmere I. Canada **50 H7** 78.00N 82.00W
El Salvador C. America **51 H2** 13.30N 89.00W
England *d.* U.K. **11 F3** 53.00N 1.00W
English Channel France/U.K. **11 F2** 50.15N 1.00W
Equatorial Guinea Africa **40 D5** 1.30N 10.30E
Erie, L. Canada/U.S.A. **50 H4** 42.15N 81.00W
Eritrea Africa **40 G6** 15.20N 38.50E
Essen Germany **18 D4** 51.27N 6.57E
Essequibo *r.* Guyana **54 F7** 6.48N 58.23W
Estonia Europe **18 F4** 58.45N 25.30E
Ethiopia Africa **40 G5** 10.00N 39.00E
Ethiopian Highlands Ethiopia **40 G6** 10.00N 37.00E
Etna, Mt. Italy **20 F2** 37.43N 14.59E
Euphrates *r.* Asia **28 D4** 31.00N 47.27E
Europe 18 - 19
Everest, Mt. Asia **29 H3** 27.59N 86.56E
Exeter England **11 E2** 50.43N 3.31W
Exminster England **11 E2** 50.41N 3.29W
Exmoor *hills* England **8 E2** 51.08N 3.45W

F

Faeroes *is.* Europe **18 C5** 62.00N 7.00W
Fair Isle Scotland **10 F6** 59.32N 1.38W
Falkland Is. S. America **55 F1** 52.00S 60.00W
Farewell, C. Greenland **50 K6** 60.00N 44.20W
Felixstowe England **11 G3** 51.58N 1.20E
Finisterre, C. Spain **18 C3** 42.54N 9.16W
Finland Europe **18 F5** 64.30N 27.00E
Finland, G. of Finland/Estonia **18 F4** 60.00N 26.50E
Firth of Clyde *est.* Scotland **10 D4** 55.35N 5.00W
Firth of Forth *est.* Scotland **10 E5** 56.05N 3.00W
Firth of Lorn *est.* Scotland **10 D5** 56.20N 5.40W
Firth of Tay *est.* Scotland **8 E4** 56.24N 3.08W
Fishguard Wales **11 D2** 51.59N 4.59W
Fleetwood England **9 E3** 53.55N 3.01W
Flinders *r.* Australia **64 E4** 15.12S 141.40E
Florence Italy **20 D5** 43.46N 11.15E
Flores *i.* Indonesia **31 E3** 8.40S 121.20E
Flores Sea Indonesia **31 D3** 7.00S 121.00E
Florianopolis Brazil **56 D2** 27.35S 48.31W
Florida, Straits of U.S.A. **48 O5** 24.00N 81.00W
Folkestone England **11 G2** 51.05N 1.11E
Forli Italy **20 E6** 44.13N 12.02E
Fortaleza Brazil **57 E4** 3.45S 38.45W
Fort William Scotland **10 D5** 56.49N 5.07W
Fort Worth U.S.A. **51 G4** 32.45N 97.20W
France Europe **18 D3** 47.00N 2.00E
Freetown Sierra Leone **40 B5** 8.30N 13.17W
French Guiana S. America **54 F7** 3.40N 53.00W
Fuji-san *mtn.* Japan **32 C3** 35.23N 138.42N
Fukuoka Japan **32 B2** 33.39N 130.21E
Fushun China **30 E8** 41.51N 123.53E
Fuzhou China **30 D6** 26.01N 119.20E

G

Gabon Africa **40 E4** 0.00 12.00E
Gaborone Botswana **41 F2** 24.45S 25.55E
Galway Rep. of Ire. **10 B3** 53.17N 9.04W
Galway B. Rep. of Ire. **10 B3** 53.12N 9.07W
Ganges *r.* India **29 H3** 23.30N 90.25E
Ganges Delta India/Bangla. **29 H3** 22.00N 89.35E
Gaoxiong Taiwan **30 E6** 22.36N 120.17E
Garda, L. Italy **20 D6** 45.40N 10.40E
Garissa Kenya **42 B2** 0.27S 39.39E
Garsen Kenya **42 C2** 2.18S 40.08E
Gaza Asia **28 C4** 31.20N 34.20E
Gdansk Poland **18 E4** 54.22N 18.38E
Geneva, L. Switz. **18 D3** 46.30N 6.30E
Georgetown Guyana **54 F7** 6.48N 58.08W
George Town Malaysia **31 C4** 5.30N 100.16E
Germany Europe **18 D4** 51.00N 10.00E
Ghana Africa **40 C5** 8.00N 1.00W
Gibraltar, Str. of Africa/Europe **18 C2** 36.00N 5.25W
Gifu Japan **32 C3** 35.27N 136.50E
Glasgow Scotland **10 D4** 55.52N 4.15W
Gloucester England **10 E2** 51.52N 2.15W
Gobi *des.* Asia **30 C8** 43.30N 103.30E
Godavari *r.* India **29 G2** 16.40N 82.15E
Godthåb *see* **Nuuk** Greenland **50**
Goiânia Brazil **56 D3** 16.43S 49.18W
Good Hope, C. of R.S.A. **41 E1** 34.20S 18.25E
Göteborg Sweden **18 E4** 57.45N 12.00E
Grampian Mts. Scotland **10 D5** 56.55N 4.00W
Gran Chaco *f.* S. America **55 E4** 23.30S 60.00W
Great Australian Bight Australia **64 C2** 33.20S 130.00E
Great Barrier Reef *f.* Australia **64 E4** 16.30S 146.30E
Great Bear L. Canada **50 E6** 66.00N 120.00W
Great Dividing Range *mts.* Australia **64 E2** 33.00S 151.00E
Great Rift Valley *f.* Africa **38 H5** 7.00S 33.00E
Great Salt L. U.S.A. **50 F4** 41.10N 112.40W
Great Sandy Desert Australia **64 C3** 21.00S 125.00E
Great Slave L. Canada **50 F6** 61.30N 114.20W
Great Victoria Desert Australia **64 C3** 29.00S 127.30E
Great Yarmouth England **11 G3** 52.36N 1.45E
Greece Europe **18 F2** 39.00N 22.00E
Green Bay *town* U.S.A. **50 H4** 44.32N 88.00W
Greenland N. America **50 K6** 68.00N 45.00W
Grenada C. America **54 E8** 12.15N 61.45W
Grimsby England **11 F3** 53.35N 0.05W
Groote Eylandt *i.* Australia **64 D4** 14.00S 136.30E
Gross Glockner *mtn.* Austria **18 E3** 47.05N 12.50E
Guadalajara Mexico **18 E3** 20.30N 103.20W
Guadeloupe C. America **54 E8** 16.20N 61.40W
Guangzhou China **30 D6** 23.20N 113.30E
Guatemala C. America **51 G3** 15.40N 90.00W
Guatemala City Guatemala **51 G2** 14.38N 90.22W
Guayaquil Ecuador **54 D6** 2.13S 79.54W
Guiana Highlands S. America **54 E7** 4.00N 59.00W
Guinea Africa **40 B6** 10.30N 10.30W
Guinea, Gulf of Africa **40 D5** 3.00N 3.00E
Guinea-Bissau Africa **40 B6** 12.00N 15.30W
Guiyang China **30 C6** 26.35N 106.40E
Guyana S. America **54 F7** 5.00N 59.00W

H

Hainan *i.* China **31 C5** 18.30N 109.40E
Hai Phong Vietnam **30 C6** 20.58N 106.41E
Haiti C. America **51 I3** 19.00N 73.00W
Hakodate Japan **32 D4** 41.46N 140.44E
Halifax Canada **50 I4** 44.38N 63.35W
Hamburg Germany **18 E4** 53.33N 10.00E
Hangzhou China **30 E7** 30.10N 120.07E
Hanoi Vietnam **30 C6** 21.01N 105.52E
Harbin China **30 E8** 45.45N 126.41E
Harris *i.* Scotland **10 C5** 57.50N 6.55W
Harrogate England **11 F3** 53.59N 1.32W
Harwich England **11 G2** 51.56N 1.18E
Hastings England **11 G2** 50.51N 0.36E
Havana Cuba **51 H3** 23.07N 82.25W
Hawaiian Is. Pacific Oc. **70 B6** 21.00N 160.00W
Helsinki Finland **18 F5** 60.08N 25.00E
Hereford England **11 E3** 52.04N 2.43W
Himalaya *mts.* Asia **29 G4** 29.00N 84.00E
Hiroshima Japan **32 B2** 34.30N 132.27E
Hispaniola *i.* C. America **48 P4** 20.00N 71.00W
Hobart Australia **64 E1** 42.54S 147.18E
Hõ Chi Minh Vietnam **31 C5** 10.46N 106.43E
Hokkaido *i.* Japan **32 D4** 43.00N 144.00E
Holyhead Wales **11 D3** 53.18N 4.38W
Honduras C. America **51 H3** 15.00N 87.00W
Honduras, G. of Carib. Sea **51 H3** 16.20N 87.30W
Hong Kong China **30 D6** 22.30N 114.10E
Honshu *i.* Japan **32 C3** 36.00N 138.00E
Horn, C. S. America **55 E1** 55.47S 67.00W
Houston U.S.A. **51 G3** 29.45N 95.25W
Huainan China **30 D7** 32.41N 117.06E
Huang He *r.* China **30 C8** 37.55N 118.46E
Huddersfield England **11 F3** 53.38N 1.49W
Hudson B. Canada **50 H5** 58.00N 86.00W
Hudson Str. Canada **50 I6** 62.00N 70.00W
Hungary Europe **18 E3** 47.30N 19.00E
Huron, L. Canada/U.S.A. **50 H5** 45.00N 82.30W

I

Ibadan Nigeria **41 D5** 7.23N 3.56E
Iceland Europe **18 B5** 64.45N 18.00W
India Asia **29 G2** 20.00N 78.00E
Indianapolis U.S.A. **51 H4** 39.45N 86.10W
Indonesia Asia **31 D3** 6.00S 118.00E
Indus *r.* Pakistan **29 F3** 24.00N 67.33E
Inn *r.* Europe **18 E3** 48.33N 13.26E
Inner Hebrides *is.* Scotland **10 C5** 56.50N 6.45W
Inverness Scotland **10 D5** 57.27N 4.15W
Ipswich England **11 G3** 52.04N 1.09E
Iran Asia **28 E4** 32.00N 54.30E
Iraq Asia **28 D4** 33.0N 44.00E
Irish Sea U.K./Rep. of Ire. **10 D3** 53.40N 5.00W
Irkutsk Russian Fed. **30 C9** 52.18N 104.15E
Irrawaddy *r.* Myanmar **29 I2** 17.45N 95.25E
Irrawaddy Delta Myanmar **29 I2** 15.30N 95.00E
Isiolo Kenya **42 B3** 0.20N 37.36E
Islamabad Pakistan 29 G4 33.40N 73.08E
Islay *i.* Scotland **10 C4** 55.45N 6.20W
Isle of Wight England **11 F2** 50.40N 1.17W
Israel Asia **28 C4** 32.00N 34.50E
Istanbul Turkey **19 F3** 41.02N 28.58E
Izmir Turkey **18 F2** 38.24N 27.09E

J

Jacksonville U.S.A. **51 H4** 30.20N 81.40W
Jakarta Indonesia **31 C3** 6.08S 106.45E
Jamaica C. America **51 H3** 18.00N 77.00W
Jamshedpur India **29 H3** 22.47N 86.12E
Japan Asia **32 C3** 36.00N 138.00E
Japan, Sea of Asia **32 B3** 40.00N 135.00E
Java *i.* Indonesia **31 C3** 7.30S 110.00E
Jayapura Indonesia **31 G3** 2.28S 140.38E
Jedda Saudi Arabia **28 C3** 21.30N 39.10E
Jerusalem Israel/Jordan **28 C4** 31.47N 35.13E
Jinan China **30 D7** 36.50N 117.00E
Jingmen China **30 D7** 31.02N 112.06E
Jodhpur India **29 G3** 26.18N 73.08E
Johannesburg R.S.A. **41 F2** 26.10S 28.02E
Jordan Asia **28 C4** 31.00N 36.00E
Jura *i.* Scotland **10 D5** 56.00N 5.55W

K

K2 *mtn.* Asia **29 G4** 35.53N 76.32E
Kabul Afghan. **29 F4** 34.30N 69.10E
Kabwe Zambia **41 F3** 14.29S 28.25E
Kagoshima Japan **32 B2** 31.37N 130.32E
Kalahari Desert Botswana **41 F2** 23.55S 23.00E
Kamchatka Pen. Russian Fed. **27 R8** 56.00N 160.00E
Kampala Uganda **40 G5** 0.19N 32.35E
Kano Nigeria **40 D6** 12.00N 8.31E
Karachi Pakistan **29 F3** 24.51N 67.02E
Kariba, L. Zimbabwe/Zambia **41 F3** 16.50S 28.00E
Kathmandu Nepal **29 H3** 27.42N 85.19E
Katowice Poland **18 E4** 50.15N 18.59E
Kattegat *str.* Denmark/Sweden **18 E4** 57.00N 11.20E
Kazakhstan Asia **28 F5** 48.00N 52.30E
Kenya Africa **42 B3** 0.00 38.00E
Kenya, Mt. Kenya **42 B2** 0.10S 37.19E
Khartoum Sudan **40 G6** 15.33N 32.35E
Kiev Ukraine **19 G4** 50.28N 30.29E
Kigali Rwanda **40 G4** 1.59S 30.05E
Kilifi Kenya **42 B2** 3.36S 39.52E
Kilimanjaro *mtn.* Tanzania **40 G4** 3.02S 37.20E
Kimberley Plateau Australia **64 C4** 17.20S 127.20E

King's Lynn England 11 G3 52.45N 0.25E
Kingston Jamaica 51 H3 17.58N 76.48W
Kingston upon Hull England 11 F3 53.45N 0.20W
Kinshasa Dem. Rep. of Congo 40 E4 4.18S 15.18E
Kirbati Pacific Oc. 71 R5 4.00S 175.00W
Kirkwall Scotland 10 E6 58.59N 2.58W
Kismaayo Somalia 40 H4 0.25S 42.31E
Kisumu Kenya 42 A2 0.03S 34.47E
Kita-Kyushu Japan 32 B2 33.50N 130.50E
Kitale Kenya 42 B3 0.59N 35.01E
Kitwe Zambia 41 F3 12.48S 28.14E
Kobe Japan 32 C2 34.42N 135.15E
Kofu Japan 32 C3 35.44N 138.34E
Kola Pen. Russian Fed. 19 G5 67.00N 38.00E
Kolyma Range mts. Russian Fed. 26 S9 63.00N 160.00E
Komatsu Japan 32 C3 36.24N 136.27E
Kosciusko, Mt. Australia 64 E2 36.28S 148.17E
Kota Bharu Malaysia 31 C4 6.07N 102.15E
Kraków Poland 18 E4 50.03N 19.55E
Kuala Lumpur Malaysia 31 C4 3.08N 101.42E
Kuching Malaysia 31 D4 1.32N 110.20E
Kumamoto Japan 32 B2 32.50N 130.42E
Kunlun Shan mts. China 29 H4 36.40N 85.00E
Kunming China 30 C6 25.04N 102.41E
Kuril Is. Russian Fed. 30 G8 46.00N 150.30E
Kushiro Japan 32 D4 42.58N 144.24E
Kuwait Asia 28 D3 29.20N 47.40E
Kuwait town Kuwait 28 D3 29.20N 48.00E
Kyoto Japan 32 C3 35.04N 135.50E
Kyrgyzstan Asia 29 G5 41.30N 75.00E
Kyushu i. Japan 32 B2 32.00N 131.00E

L
Laayoune W. Sahara 40 B7 27.10N 13.11W
Labrador f. Canada 50 I5 54.00N 61.30W
Ladoga, L. Russian Fed. 19 G5 61.00N 32.00E
Lagan r. N. Ireland 11 C4 54.37N 5.54W
Lagos Nigeria 40 D5 6.27N 3.28E
Lahore Pakistan 29 G4 31.34N 74.22E
Lake District England 11 E4 54.30N 3.10W
Lamu Kenya 42 A2 2.20S 40.54E
Lancaster England 11 E4 54.03N 2.48W
Land's End c. England 11 D2 50.03N 5.45W
Lanzhou China 30 C7 36.01N 103.45E
Laos Asia 30 C6 19.00N 104.00E
La Paz Bolivia 54 E5 16.30S 68.10W
Lappland f. Sweden/Finland 16 F5 68.10N 24.00E
Larne N. Ireland 11 D4 54.51N 5.50W
Latvia Europe 18 F4 57.00N 25.00E
Lebanon Asia 28 C4 34.00N 36.00E
Leeds England 11 F3 53.48N 1.34W
Le Havre France 18 D3 49.30N 0.06E
Leicester England 11 F3 52.39N 1.09W
Leipzig Germany 18 E4 51.20N 12.20E
Lena r. Russian Fed. 26 O9 72.00N 127.10E
Lerwick Scotland 10 F7 60.09N 1.09W
Lesotho Africa 41 F2 29.30S 28.00E
Lewis i. Scotland 10 C6 58.10N 6.40W
Lhasa China 29 I3 29 41N 91.10E
Liberia Africa 40 C5 6.30N 9.30W
Libreville Gabon 40 E4 0.30N 9.25E
Libya Africa 40 E7 26.30N 17.00E
Libyan Desert Africa 40 F7 23.00N 26.10E
Liechtenstein Europe 18 D3 47.08N 9.35E
Liffey r. Rep. of Ire. 11 C3 53.21N 6.14W
Ligurian Sea Med. Sea 20 C5 43.10N 9.00E
Likasi Dem. Rep. of Congo 40 F3 10.58S 26.47E
Lille France 18 D4 50.39N 3.05E
Lilongwe Malawi 40 G3 13.58S 33.49E
Lima Peru 54 D5 12.06S 77.03W
Limerick Rep. of Ire. 11 B3 52.40N 8.37W
Limpopo r. Mozambique 41 F2 25.14S 33.33E
Lincoln England 11 F3 53.14N 0.32W
Lions, G. of France 18 D3 43.00N 4.15E
Lisbon Portugal 18 C2 38.44N 9.08W
Lithuania Europe 18 F4 55.00N 24.00E
Liupanshui China 30 C6 26.50N 104.45E
Liuzhou China 30 C6 24.17N 109.15E
Liverpool England 11 E3 53.25N 3.00W
Livorno Italy 20 D5 43.33N 10.18E
Ljubljana Slovenia 18 E3 46.04N 14.28E
Llanos f. Colombia/Venezuela 54 D7 5.30N 72.00W
Łódz Poland 18 E4 51.49N 19.28E
Logan, Mt. Canada 50 D6 60.45N 140.00W
Loire r. France 18 D3 47.18N 2.00W
Lomé Togo 40 D5 6.10N 1.21E
Lomond, Loch Scotland 10 D5 56.07N 4.36W
London England 11 F2 51.32N 0.06W
Londonderry N. Ireland 10 C4 55.00N 7.20W
Los Angeles U.S.A. 48 F5 34.00N 118.17W
Lower California pen. Mexico 51 F3 27.00N 113.00W
Lower Lough Erne N. Ireland 11 C4 54.28N 7.48W
Luanda Angola 40 E4 8.50S 13.20E
Lüderitz Namibia 41 E2 26.38S 15.10E
Lule r. Sweden 18 F5 65.40N 21.48E

Luoyang China 30 D7 34.48N 112.25E
Lusaka Zambia 41 F3 15.26S 28.20E
Luton England 11 F2 51.53N 0.25W
Luxembourg Europe 18 D3 49.50N 6.15E
Luxembourg town Lux. 18 D3 49.37N 6.08E
Luzon i. Phil. 31 E5 17.50N 121.00E
Lyon France 18 D3 45.46N 4.50E

M
Macapá Brazil 56 C5 0.01N 51.01W
Macau Asia 30 D6 22.13N 113.36E
Macedonia Europe 18 F3 41.15N 21.15E
Maceió Brazil 57 E4 9.34S 35.47W
Mackenzie r. Canada 50 E7 69.20N 134.00W
Madagascar Africa 41 H3 20.00S 46.30E
Madeira i. Atlantic Oc. 38 C9 32.45N 17.00W
Madras see Chennai India 29
Madre Occidental, Sierra mts. Mexico 51 F3 25.00N 105.00W
Madre Oriental, Sierra mts. Mexico 51 G3 24.00N 101.00W
Madrid Spain 17 C3 40.25N 3.43W
Madurai India 29 G1 9.55N 78.07E
Magellan, Str. of Chile 55 D1 53.00S 71.00W
Maggiore, L. Italy 20 C7 46.00N 8.37E
Makran f. Asia 28 E3 25.40N 62.00E
Malabo Equat. Guinea 40 D5 3.45N 8.48E
Malawi Africa 41 G3 13.00S 34.00E
Malaysia Asia 31 C4 5.00N 110.00E
Maldives Indian Oc. 26 J3 6.20N 73.00E
Mali Africa 40 C6 16.00N 3.00W
Mallorca i. Spain 18 D2 39.35N 3.00E
Malta Europe 18 E2 35.55N 14.25E
Man, Isle of U.K. 11 D4 54.15N 4.30W
Managua Nicaragua 51 H2 12.06N 86.18W
Manaus Brazil 56 C4 3.06S 60.00W
Manchester England 11 E3 53.30N 2.15W
Manchuria f. Asia 30 E8 45.00N 125.00E
Mandalay Myanmar 29 I3 21.57N 96.04E
Mangalore India 29 G2 12.54N 74.51E
Manila Phil. 31 E5 14.36N 120.59E
Manizales Colombia 54 D7 5.03N 75.32W
Mantua Italy 20 D6 45.09N 10.47E
Maoke Range mts. Indonesia 31 F3 4.00S 137.30E
Maputo Mozambique 41 G2 25.58S 32.35E
Maraca, Ilha de i. Brazil 56 D4 2.00N 50.30W
Maracaibo Venezuela 54 D8 10.44N 71.37W
Marañón r. Peru 54 D6 4.00S 73.30W
Mar del Plata Argentina 55 F3 38.00S 57.32W
Marakesh Morocco 40 C8 31.49N 8.00W
Marsabit Kenya 42 B3 2.20N 37.59E
Marseille France 18 D3 43.18N 5.22E
Maseru Lesotho 41 F2 29.19S 27.29E
Mashhad Iran 28 E4 36.16N 59.34E
Massif Central mts. France 18 D3 45.00N 3.30E
Matera Italy 20 G4 40.41N 16.36E
Mato Grosso, Planalto do f. Brazil 56 C3 15.00S 55.00W
Mauritania Africa 40 B6 20.00N 10.00W
Mauritius Indian Oc. 71 L4 20.10S 58.00E
Mbabane Swaziland 41 G2 26.20S 31.08E
McKinley, Mt. U.S.A. 50 C6 63.00N 151.00W
Mecca Saudi Arabia 28 C3 21.26N 39.49E
Medan Indonesia 31 B4 3.35N 98.39E
Medellin Colombia 54 D7 6.15N 75.36W
Medina Saudi Arabia 28 C3 24.30N 39.35E
Mediterranean Sea 16 D2
Mekong r. Asia 31 C5 10.00N 106.20E
Melbourne Australia 64 E2 37.45S 144.58E
Mendoza Argentina 55 E3 33.00S 68.52W
Menorca i. Spain 18 D2 40.00N 4.00e
Merano Italy 20 D7 46.41N 11.10E
Mersey r. England 11 E3 53.22N 2.37W
Meru Kenya 42 B3 0.03N 37.38E
Messina Italy 20 F3 38.13N 15.34E
Mexico C. America 51 G3 20.00N 100.00W
Mexico, G. of N. America 51 G3 25.00N 90.00W
Mexico City Mexico 51 G3 19.25N 99.10W
Miami-Fort Lauderdale U.S.A. 51 H3 25.45N 80.10W
Michigan U.S.A. 50 H4 44.00N 87.00W
Middlesbrough England 11 F4 54.34N 1.13W
Milan Italy 20 C6 45.28N 9.16E
Milwaukee U.S.A. 50 H4 43.03N 87.56W
Mindanao i. Phil. 31 E5 7.30N 125.00E
Mindoro i. Phil. 31 E5 13.00N 121.00E
Minneapolis-St. Paul U.S.A. 50 G5 45.00N 93.15W
Minsk Belarus 18 F4 53.51N 27.30E
Mississippi r. U.S.A. 50 G4 28.55N 89.05W
Missouri r. U.S.A. 50 G5 38.40N 90.20W
Mito Japan 32 D3 36.30N 140.24E
Modena Italy 20 D6 44.39N 10.55E
Mogadishu Somalia 40 H5 2.02N 45.21E
Moldova Europe 18 F3 47.30N 28.30E
Mombasa Kenya 42 B2 4.04S 39.40E
Monaco Europe 18 D3 43.40N 7.25E
Mongolia Asia 30 C8 46.30N 104.00E

Monrovia Liberia 40 B5 6.20N 10.46W
Monterrey Mexico 51 G3 25.40N 100.20W
Montevideo Uruguay 55 F3 34.55S 56.10W
Montréal Canada 50 I5 45.30N 73.36W
Monza Italy 20 C6 45.35N 9.16E
Moray Firth est. Scotland 10 E5 57.45N 3.50W
Morecambe B. England 11 E3 54.05N 3.00W
Morocco Africa 40 C8 31.00N 5.00W
Morpeth England 10 F4 55.10N 1.40W
Moscow Russian Fed. 19 G4 55.45N 37.42E
Mosul Iraq 28 D4 36.21N 43.08E
Moulmein Myanmar 29 I2 16.20N 97.50E
Mourne Mts. N. Ireland 11 C4 54.10N 6.02W
Mozambique Africa 40 G3 18.00S 35.00E
Mozambique Channel Indian Oc. 40 H3 16.00S 42.30E
Mull i. Scotland 10 D5 56.28N 5.56W
Mumbai India 29 G2 18.56N 72.51E
Munich Germany 18 E3 48.08N 11.35E
Mureş r. Romania 18 F3 46.16N 20.10E
Murray r. Australia 64 D2 35.23S 139.20E
Muscat Oman 28 E3 23.36N 58.37E
Mweru, L. Zambia/Dem. Rep. of Congo 40 F4 9.00S 28.40E
Myanmar Asia 29 I3 21.00N 95.00E

N
Nacala Mozambique 41 H3 14.30S 40.3E
Nagasaki Japan 32 A2 32.45N 129.52E
Nagoya Japan 32 C3 35.08N 136.53E
Nairobi Kenya 42 B2 1.17S 36.50E
Nakuru Kenya 42 B2 0.16S 36.04E
Namib Desert Namibia 41 E2 22.50S 14.40E
Namibia Africa 41 E2 22.00S 17.00E
Nanjing China 30 D7 32.00N 118.40E
Nanning China 30 C6 22.50N 108.19E
Nantes France 18 C3 47.14N 1.35W
Naples Italy 20 F4 40.50N 14.14E
Narmada r. India 26 J5 21.40N 73.00E
Nasser, L. Egypt 40 G7 22.40N 32.00E
Natal Brazil 57 E4 5.46S 35.15W
Nauru Pacific Oc. 71 R5 0.32S 166.55E
Ndjamena Chad 40 E6 12.10N 14.59E
Ndola Zambia 41 F3 13.00S 28.39E
Neagh, Lough N. Ireland 11 C4 54.36N 6.26W
Negro r. Brazil 56 B4 3.30S 60.00W
Nepal Asia 29 H3 28.00N 84.00E
Ness, Loch Scotland 10 D5 57.16N 4.30W
Netherlands Europe 18 D4 52.00N 5.30E
Netherlands Antilles is. S. America 54 E8 12.30N 69.00W
Nevada, Sierra mts. U.S.A. 48 K6 37.30N 119.00W
New Caledonia i. Pacific Oc. 65 G3 22.00S 165.00E
Newcastle upon Tyne England 11 F4 54.58N 1.36W
New Delhi India 29 G3 28.37N 77.13E
Newfoundland i. Canada 50 J5 48.30N 56.00W
New Guinea i. Austa. 64 E5 5.00S 140.00E
Newhaven England 11 G2 50.46N 0.07E
New Orleans U.S.A. 51 G3 30.00N 90.03W
Newport Wales 11 E2 51.34N 2.59W
New Siberian Is. Russian Fed. 26 Q10 76.00N 144.00E
New York U.S.A. 50 I4 40.40N 73.50W
New Zealand Austa. 64 H1 41.00S 175.00E
Niamey Niger 40 D6 13.32N 2.05E
Nicaragua C. America 51 H2 13.00N 85.00W
Nicaragua, L. Nicaragua 48 O4 11.30N 85.30W
Nicobar Is. India 31 I1 8.00N 94.00E
Niger Africa 40 D6 17.00N 10.00E
Niger r. Nigeria 40 D6 4.15N 6.05E
Nigeria Africa 40 D6 9.00N 9.00E
Nile r. Egypt 40 G7 31.30N 30.25E
Nîmes France 18 D3 43.50N 4.21E
North America 48
Northampton England 11 F3 52.14N 0.54W
North C. Norway 16 F6 71.10N 25.45E
North Channel U.K. 10 D4 55.00N 5.30W
Northern Ireland d. U.K. 11 C4 54.40N 6.45W
North European Plain f. Europe 16 F4 56.00N 27.00E
North I. New Zealand 65 H2 39.00S 175.00E
North Korea Asia 30 E8 40.00N 128.00E
North Sea Europe 18 D4 56.00N 4.00E
North Uist i. Scotland 10 C5 57.35N 7.20W
North York Moors hills England 11 F4 54.21N 0.50W
Norway Europe 18 D5 65.00N 13.00E
Norwegian Sea Europe 18 D5 66.00N 2.00E
Nottingham England 11 F3 52.57N 1.10W
Nouakchott Mauritania 40 B6 18.09N 15.58W
Nova Iguaçu Brazil 57 D2 22.45S 43.27W
Novaya Zemlya i. Russian Fed. 26 H10 74.00N 56.00E
Nubian Desert Sudan 40 G7 21.00N 34.00E
Nullarbor Plain f. Australia 64 C2 31.30S 128.00E
Nuuk Greenland 50 J6 64.10N 51.40W
Nyasa, L. Africa 40 G3 12.00S 34.30E

O
Ob r. Russian Fed. 26 I9 66.50N 69.00E
Oban Scotland 10 D5 56.26N 5.28W
Oder r. Poland/Germany 18 E4 53.30N 14.36E
Odessa Ukraine 19 G3 46.30N 30.46E
Ohio r. U.S.A. 51 H4 37.07N 89.10W
Okavango Delta Botswana 41 F2 19.30S 23.00E
Okayama Japan 32 B2 34.40N 133.54E
Oldham England 11 E3 53.33N 2.08W
Olympus mtn. Cyprus 19 G2 34.55N 32.52E
Oman Asia 28 E2 22.30N 57.30E
Oman, G. of Asia 28 E3 25.00N 58.00E
Onega, L. Russian Fed. 19 G5 62.00N 35.30E
Ontario, L. Canada/U.S.A. 50 H4 43.40N 78.00W
Oporto Portugal 18 C3 41.09N 8.37W
Orange r. R.S.A. 41 E2 28.43S 16.30E
Orinoco r. Venezuela 54 E7 9.00N 61.30W
Orinoco Delta r. Venezuela 54 E7 9.00N 61.30W
Orkney Is. Scotland 10 E6 59.00N 3.00W
Osaka Japan 32 C2 34.40N 135.30E
Oslo Norway 18 E4 59.56N 10.45E
Ottawa Canada 50 H5 45.25N 75.43W
Ougadougou Burkina 40 C6 12.20N 1.40W
Ouse r. England 11 F3 53.41N 0.42W
Outer Hebrides is. Scotland 10 C5 58.00N 7.35W
Owen Stanley Range mts. P.N.G. 64 E5 9.30S 148.00E
Oxford England 11 F2 51.45N 1.15W
Ozark Plateau U.S.A. 48 N6 36.00N 93.35W

P
Pacific Ocean 68 C6
Padua Italy 20 D6 45.27N 11.52E
Pakistan Asia 28 F3 30.00N 70.00E
Palau Pacific Oc. 31 F4 7.00N 134.25E
Palembang Indonesia 31 C3 2.59S 104.50E
Palermo Italy 20 E3 38.09N 13.22E
Palmerston North New Zealand 65 H1 40.21S 175.37E
Pampas f. Argentina 55 E3 35.00S 63.00W
Panama C.America 51 H2 9.00N 80.00W
Panama Canal Panama 51 H2 9.21N 79.54W
Panama City Panama 51 H2 8.57N 79.30W
Panay i. Phil. 31 E5 11.10N 122.30E
Papua New Guinea Austa. 64 E5 6.00S 148.00E
Paraguay S. America 55 F4 23.00S 58.00W
Paraguay r. Argentina 55 F4 27.30S 58.50W
Paramaribo Suriname 54 F7 5.52N 55.14W
Paraná r. Argentina 55 F4 34.00S 58.30W
Paranaiba r. Brazil 56 C3 20.00S 51.00W
Paris France 18 D3 48.52N 2.20E
Patagonia f. Argentina 55 E2 45.00S 68.00W
Patna India 29 H3 25.37N 85.12E
Patras Greece 18 F2 38.15N 21.45E
Peipus, L. Europe 18 F4 58.30N 27.30E
Pembroke Wales 11 D2 51.41N 4.57W
Penzance England 11 D2 50.07N 5.32W
Perth Australia 64 B2 31.58S 115.49E
Perth Scotland 10 E5 56.24N 3.28W
Peru S. America 54 D5 10.00S 75.00W
Pescara Italy 20 F5 42.27N 14.13E
Peshawar Pakistan 29 G4 34.01N 71.40E
Peterborough England 11 F3 52.35N 0.14W
Philadelphia U.S.A. 50 H4 39.55N 75.10W
Philippines Asia 31 E5 13.00N 123.00E
Phnom Penh Cambodia 31 C5 11.35N 104.55E
Pindus Mts. Albania/Greece 18 F2 39.40N 21.00E
Pittsburgh U.S.A. 50 H4 40.26N 79.58W
Plymouth England 11 D2 50.23N 4.09W
Poland Europe 18 E4 52.30N 19.00E
Poole England 11 F2 50.42N 1.58W
Popocatépetl mtn. Mexico 51 G3 19.02N 98.38W
Port-au-Prince Haiti 51 I3 18.33N 72.20W
Port Moresby P.N.G. 64 E5 9.30S 147.07E
Pörto Alegre Brazil 56 C1 30.03S 51.10W
Port of Spain Trinidad 54 E8 10.38N 61.31W
Porto-Novo Benin 40 D5 6.30N 2.47E
Porto Velho Brazil 56 B4 8.45S 63.54W
Portsmouth England 11 F2 50.48N 1.06W
Portugal Europe 18 C2 39.30N 8.05W
Poznan Poland 18 E4 52.25N 16.53E
Prague Czech Rep. 18 E4 50.05N 14.25E
Preston England 11 E3 53.46N 2.42W
Pretoria R.S.A. 41 F2 25.45S 28.12E
Prince of Wales I. Canada 50 G7 73.00N 99.00W
Puerto Rico C. America 51 I3 18.20N 66.30W
Puncak Jaya mtn. Indonesia 31 F3 4.00S 137.15E
Pune India 29 G2 18.34N 73.58E
Purus r. Brazil 56 B4 3.15S 61.30W
Pusan S. Korea 30 E7 35.05N 129.02E
Pyongyang N. Korea 30 E7 39.00N 125.47E
Pyrenees mts. France/Spain 18 D3 42.40N 0.30E

Q
Qatar Asia 28 E3 25.20N 51.10E
Qattara Depression f. Egypt 40 F7 30.00N 27.30E